JUST DON'T FORGET ME

Picture Index

Page 51	BJ, 2 weeks before turning 4
Page 122	Feb 2013 with Tyler Nathaniel Enloe Galveston Fieldtrip
Page 132	BJ with older brother Michael, summer 2012
Page 145	Nick, BJ and Kelli, July 2013
Page 177	BJ, 5 months, 5 days old
Page 241	Kimberly Ann Cutler
Back Cover	Sirius Fuentes, Michael Crawford (BJ's older brother), Ronnie Grimes

JUST DON'T FORGET ME

KIMBERLY A. CUTLER

Idea Creations Press
www.ideacreationspress.com

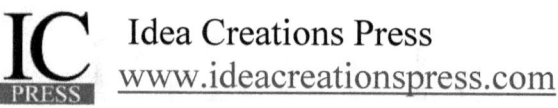 Idea Creations Press
www.ideacreationspress.com

Copyright © Kimberly A. Cutler, 2015.

All rights reserved. No part of this book may be reproduced or transmitted in any form or by any means, electronic or mechanical, including photocopying, recording, or by an information storage and retrieval system, without permission in writing from the author.

Although this book is primarily non-fiction, approximately 5% is fiction. The non-fictional characters that have been chosen to make fiction have no resemblance to actual persons, though the stories behind them are true. All other names and photos in this book have been used with written permission.

Library of Congress Control Number: 2015939387

ISBN-13: 978-0988810785
ISBN-10: 0988810786

Printed in the U.S.A.

"Kim, a devoted and loving mother, has shared with us a tender and heartfelt tribute to her son, BJ. The loss of a child is inconceivable and traumatic. She expresses the unspeakable heartache, grief and despair surrounding this loss. Witty and articulate, at one moment Kim has us laughing out loud at the antics of her son. And in the next, we weep with her as she shares her loss. Through her journey is revealed a very strong woman of faith. One gets the feeling that BJ is smiling down on her, well-pleased with his mother's beautiful tribute to him."

Terri Russell
ASEA Associate and licensed social worker

"BJ's Story by Kim Cutler is a wonderful story that explains her undying love of a child, including faith and hope for her son BJ and the joy and happiness of being close to BJ as his mother - gathering in grand adventures along the way.

Kim shares the stories with us of BJ's childhood up to the heartache of her loss. BJ's Story is a collection of stories that will help other parents cope with the loss of a child knowing they are not alone during this sad time. This is truly a wonderful book about a mother's loss of a child, a child that left this world too soon, and her faith that has helped her through it."

Nikki Jackson
Sales associate at Hydra Tan Salon

"Kim shares her joys of motherhood and the difficulties of managing it both single and with the romance of finding the loves in her life. As the story evolves, she shares the broken pieces of her heart during the weeks and days leading up to one of the hardest moments no parent should have to experience, while allowing readers an insight into what she has lived through and learned from to help her move on.

I believe BJ's Story will be most appreciated by those who are suffering through their own loss of a child. They may find comfort in knowing that they are not alone in their thoughts and feelings during their trying time. Others may appreciate this heartfelt tribute of one mother's suffering and faith and the courage needed to move on."

Kristy Wilson
Kristy@RunawayBridalPlanner

"Do you know the sum of your strength? Kim Cutler has shared from within her heart, wonderful, yet heartbreaking moments of her son BJ. We hear memories from his birth to his adolescence and teenage years, then to his devastating diagnosis.

I highly recommend this book because it is an inspiring story of faith, dedication, as well as heartaches endured along the way."

Jennifer Hoppas Hyde
Loan Officer at United Energy Credit Union

For BJ

We all have to lose loved ones. We all have to die ourselves knowing in Christ we will live again. I know I shall be reunited with my son BJ in God's time. Until then, he'll be the angel on my shoulder. I love you BJ with all of my heart.

    I hope this book helps others to know you and of those who knew you, to remember you forever. But then, how could anyone ever forget someone like you?

    Forever in Our Hearts <3
    Love, Mom

For All Whom BJ Loved

Facebook Post:
*October 26, 2011**

"I hope you'll all remember me well. As a good friend, as a nice guy, or jsut as the kid who made you laugh, I love all of you guys. Even the random people who I just click 'accept' because we have some mutual friends. I'm not going to be around for forever, and I just want you all to know that you're awesome. I don't know if there is a god, or what he has in store for me, but the way things have been going so far, he doesn't seem to like me too much. I'll stick around for all of you guys, and in return, just don't forget me..."

(This is the Facebook post that inspired this book to be written in his honor. He never wanted to be forgotten!!! Love you BJ <3 < 3 <3)

*This and all future Facebook inclusions from BJ are in their original text. No correction of grammar or sentence structure has been made.

Special Thanks

I would especially like to thank Scott Tatum for sharing stories of himself with BJ regarding Pokémon' tournaments in Indiana at a time I was no longer married to his father, which gave me memories I otherwise would never have known, and also BJ's older brother Michael Crawford who also shared on BJ's many levels of maturity of spirit at such a young age. He gave me insight to things which mattered most to him, things that most people trample under their feet but have been known to man since the beginning of time, all to be forgotten by modernization.

Michael helped me to see that BJ was a young boy with wisdom beyond his years in many facets. He told me stories I had no clue about; he knew how complex this young boy's thinking in reality was.

Without their contribution this book wouldn't have been possible. I'd like to also thank those who gave permission to have their names used in my book and their stories about their adventure's with BJ… special thanks to each and every one for making his dream a reality!

"I'll stick around for all of you guys, and in return, just don't forget me."

May he never be forgotten and may his legacy live on in our hearts forever! We love you Benjamin Forrest Crawford!

December 15, 1995 to July 9, 2013

Missing You

I miss you more each passing day and wonder where you are. Do you see my tears of sorrow as I stare up at the stars?

Do you walk beside me on a cold and windy day, or are you the rustle of the leaves that gently blow away?

I wonder if you show me signs that you are by my side. There are times I feel your presence and it's much too strong to hide.

I often find the tears are streaming down my face, I wonder if you're with me then or in another place.

Do you hear the words I speak as I talk to you? The silly memories that I share, the joys and laughter, too?

Do you hear me when my soul is empty and I feel I can't go on? For those are the hardest moments, when I know you're really gone.

I wish somehow, somewhere, someday, together we could meet. If only for a moment to walk along the street.

For just another chance to say how much I care. To say how much I love you, how I always will be there.

I wonder where you are as I sit upon the shore. I listen to the waves but hear your voice no more.

If only you could talk to me for just another day, I'd tell you that I love you, then what would you say?

So as I walk away, and so unknown to me I leave behind two butt prints in the sand along the sea.

The Other Side

If only we could take a glimpse of the other side. All our grieving pain and sorrow would be washed away by the tide.

The souls of men are many even more than the sand of the sea. God brought us to this earthly life so that we might understand and believe.

Every person ever born that came into this world, one day must surely die. For immortal men are we.

This life is just a test to see if we will do his will, and keep all of his promises just like we said we will.

We have no recollection of what life was before. God gently hugged us good-bye, and then we were born.

So into sin and sorrow sometimes lost to find our way. Often the help from others who God chooses to place in our way. And so we must rely on faith and truly believe. And when a loved one dies, know that it's OK to grieve.

Just don't let it consume you, or occupy your day. Or turn your heart to bitterness, for Satan would have it that way.

Just grab hold of the iron rod and hold on with your might. Trust your Heavenly Father that all will be alright.

Our loved ones are not far away but closer now than ever. And when it comes our turn to die we'll walk through the veil together.

Prologue:
The Essence of BJ

by Michael Crawford, BJ's older brother,
with additional comments from the author

To make a long story short I suppose, I will show you some of the things BJ showed me. After introducing me to the documentary "The Secret Life of Plants" I began to consider seriously, for the first time in my life, the unity of all existence. We are all part of the same universal Christ-like consciousness. As my confidence in this newfound spirituality grew, we kept learning and sharing more and more information with each other.

I remember one day showing him a video of a girl who described the importance of maintaining a gland in your brain called the pineal gland. You may know it as the *third eye* from many different cultures. But, the significance of this gland is a big one that mostly goes ignored. The third eye is our connection to this "consciousness," and it has been misused and mistreated to the point that it has shrunken in size from an eyeball to hardly that of a raisin.

From there we began searching natural remedies for illness, deficiencies, and disease of which cancer was an amazingly popular subject with so much positive support, support for some reason or another, BJ and I both seemed to neglect during the last few months of his life. (This subject is a bit hard for me to talk about because it makes me regret how I spent my time while BJ was in the hospital).

From here BJ showed me something truly jaw dropping; a compilation of many new age ideas in the form of a series of short information films. One of them was called, *Crystal Science Video #13*. The Spirit Science videos, while pretty out of this world, opened my eyes to SO many possibilities. Were we Gods? Is the idea of life outside earth truly as bizarre as society would lead me to believe? You get the idea.

After showing me the Crystal Science videos, he obtained a few pocket stones, (called Kacha stones or healing stones, which are crystals and gem stones with healing powers; the series of *Spirit Science #13* refers to this in particular) from his friends with mood and perspective altering abilities. The first one he gave me was a turquoise; I will never forget its shape. I actually still have every one of them.

Basically, I was lost at a time in my life. I had no direction, no purpose, and a pretty despicable view of the world around me. BJ opened my eyes to the higher possibilities, he made me truly appreciate every living moment I spend and every action I take. I wish I only knew how to thank him properly.

- Michael Crawford

***

All of these healing methods have been known by man since the beginning of time. Some have been known by a few seekers, but rarely by a boy just seventeen-years-old. He was truly an old soul in a young body, who knew more about the universe and how various matters functioned than most adults might ever comprehend.

    Although I was unaware of it at the time, Michael told me that all of his friends had brought their pocket stones up to the hospital when he was sick. They'd placed them around his bed, hoping for spiritual healing, a healing which never came.

    Apparently the God of the universe had other plans...but his spirit lives on, and the lives he has touched and changed will continue to have a ripple effect for good.

Magical Things

So many times you held him when he was just a boy, filled with all the magical things of life for him to enjoy.

Before you opened your eyes he was already grown then Heavenly Father had called him home. Now all that is left is you, you alone.

Sweet memories linger that won't go away, you closed your eyes and then opened them one day. Now everything dear God has taken away. And oh how you wished he could stay.

You sit in the dark and try to comprehend, no more holding back, no more trying to pretend, reality now has finally set in he is gone.

How could a God so loving and fare just leave you to linger alone in despair? Heavenly Father has called him home, all that is left now is you, you alone.

All your friends tell you it will be OK so you hold on tight to every word that they say. You hope and you dream and you even pray. You closed your eyes and then opened them one day. Now everything dear God has taken away.

Then suddenly a vision comes into your mind. That boy who had grown to a man you did find. Then God shows you part of His great plan divine, and you're still.

He shows you how he is no longer in pain. How life he enjoys in the Kingdom he reigns, victorious boy who you once called your own son.

How blessed a woman you must have been, for God to have chosen you to look after him, during his days as a mortal child on this earth. How could you ever have known when you gave him birth.

What royalty lived within your own womb, from a Father you thought took him home way too soon.

Now he rules and reigns with the Kings up above, and with all his heart he sends you his love, your guardian angel from up above. He always will love you so go ahead shout, things happen for a reason so don't ever doubt. The magical things in this life are now left for you to enjoy now.

So go ahead and be happy, go ahead and enjoy, and thank your Heavenly Father for that sweet baby boy. Sometimes we cannot see the whole picture so God gives us a sample, what a glorious way to set an example.

***Facebook Post:
December 11, 2011***

"What a great morning to be alive"

Once Upon a Time

It began long ago with my own birth; I was born in Pasadena, California, September 27, 1962. I was born and raised as a Jehovah's Witness, until we moved from Southern California, up to Northern California when I was ten-years-old. I was a bit young to grasp then what this religion really offered or believed in.

However, I do remember what it didn't believe in, and to a young child that seemed like just about everything. This included all holidays, birthdays, saluting the flag, or celebrations of any kind. We were never allowed to participate in holiday events such as Christmas parties, etc. We sat alone in rooms by ourselves while others enjoyed them and we wondered what we had done wrong to deserve this, speaking for myself anyway. I always felt "different" and never quite fit in so when we stopped going to church and moved from the Los Angeles, California area up to Redding, California, I have to admit I was quite relieved.

I did not fit in as traditional schools in Southern California made you wear dresses unless it rained. Up north was like a different state. Everything from the people and the culture to, unfortunately, the clothes. So again, I did not fit in. I stood out like a fish out of water, with no pants to my name, and was made fun of a lot.

By age fifteen I had discovered bulimia. I truly believed I was the only person in the world who had ever made themselves vomit, until I saw a TV show about it. This would remain one of my life challenges for many years to come. I married at age eighteen and had my oldest daughter at age nineteen, and my next daughter at just twenty-one.

I soon found myself a single mother with two small children. I had started smoking at the young age of twelve and had quit at age twenty-five. At this time my then controlled eating disorder came back full force. It was my substitute for smoking. It was my addiction replacement which nearly destroyed me. I was losing my hair and I also lost my ability to procreate for three full years. Although single at the time, I knew one day I would want to remarry and have more children. I went to a doctor from a church I had joined at age twenty-five and he tried everything humanly possible to get me back on track yet nothing seemed to work. I was finally told I would never be able to have more children and left his office devastated.

I prayed and fasted a lot and one day received a miracle. I became regular as clockwork every twenty-eight days. Although a bit of a touchy subject, it is also a very natural one and I like to think of it as a "very special gift." Most women refer to it as "The Curse" each month, but I truly believe it to be a gift from God. It is our ability to procreate and become more like our Father in Heaven. How can that *not* be a gift?

So there it all began on one cold winter's day. It was December 15, 1995. Thank goodness for C-sections. My first daughter came after 22 ½ hours of labor with no pain meds whatsoever after my water broke. Then a surprise C-section with each of my following five children as well, and I welcomed them.

We lived in a small town in Northern California named Ukiah. Ukiah is of Indian origin meaning "Deep Valley."

Ukiah is a small town. In 1996, Ukiah was ranked the #1 best small town to live in California and the sixth-best place to live in the United States. The population was 16,075 at the 2010 census. It is located 120 miles north of San Francisco in a crossroads of the wine country and redwoods. The seat of Mendocino County, it sits as one of the few towns in what is a lush agricultural area.

Ukiah is also an epicenter of progressive politics--well known for its decriminalization of marijuana and the ban of genetically modified organisms. However, there is also a significant conservative population as well.

While Ukiah has been blessed with beauty, with the closure of several logging and industrial companies, jobs are often hard to find. At the same time, the wide appeal of Ukiah's small-town charm and the slow but steady sprawl of the Bay Area have made housing prices high for an area of its size and isolation.

After living eighteen years in Redding, California, I moved with my two young daughters, ages six and nine, to be closer to my mom. They had grown up with her, and we really had no other family in Redding we were close to. It was a hard decision to leave their dad, but if we stayed they would also miss their grandma who they loved. After months of debating and much prayer, we decided to move, knowing they would still be able to come back and visit their dad often.

It was in 1987, in Redding, California, that I had joined another church that I still belong to. Growing up in another religion from birth to age ten taught me to believe in a God. Even though I was much too young to grasp what their basic beliefs were, nor did I later accept them, I found a church while living in Redding where all the puzzle pieces seemed to fit and where I continue to go to this day.

I don't like being referred to as a religious person, in fact that would probably be offensive to me. However, if someone were to say I was a spiritual person, I would take that as a compliment. I believe out of all the many, many religions out there, most of them have a lot of good to offer, some more than others. I like the quote that, "We are spiritual beings having a mortal experience vs. mortal beings having a spiritual experience."

Whenever a person can find a power greater than themselves, a God of their understanding, then more power to them. I grew up with the same God as a child that I have today, although a different religion. My God has changed and evolved and continues to change as I am learning to trust Him, turn my will and life over to Him and remember that He is in charge. That He can do for me the things I cannot do for myself. That without Him I am nothing. With Him, all things are possible and there is nothing I cannot do. I don't want to sound preachy throughout my book nor do I want to offend anyone, so when I say God just think God as you understand Him, or a Higher Power greater than yourself, Spirit of the Universe, or whatever. I just choose to call mine, God, or my Father in Heaven, as I believe He is the father of my spirit just as my earthly father is the father of my physical body.

Meanwhile, in Ukiah, I loved the apartment layout but hated everything that went along with it. There were cockroaches everywhere. My kids would go to brush their teeth and find them on their toothbrushes. I'd serve them a meal, only to find one on the very plate of food I was serving them.

A neighbor would sit near his window and expose himself to children as they walked by. There would be gang fights and shootings in the center of the apartment complex. I remember a time when my pregnant neighbor and I went out to see what all the commotion was about and were politely escorted back to our apartments by the police and told not to leave our apartments again for at least twelve hours.

Upstairs the neighbors had a lot of drug traffic and all kinds of people would come and go all hours of the day or night. Next to them, a couple of Hispanic families all lived in the one apartment. Often you would find one member of that family in the parking lot throwing up from drinking too much alcohol. The swimming pool was filled with sand.

My mom had chosen this apartment complex for me as it was in my budget, being on welfare at the time, and I hadn't seen it before I moved in. The low-income apartment I could afford had a two year waiting list; sadly, it was so bad my girls were not allowed to play outside for safety reasons. Ukiah is a very friendly little town but this apartment complex was drug-related, crime-related, and just plain not a good place to be.

After a few months in a small city I decided to move back to Redding. A couple friends of mine, Eddie and Kate, came with me. I collected as many apartment applications as I could, knowing that I would fill them out later and send them in by mail. We went all day as it got up to 104 degrees and my car at that time had no air conditioning so we made the best of a miserable situation, stopping many times to drink or to eat. Due to our many stops, we accumulated a lot of garbage after we had emptied bottles of soda and various food items. We eventually stopped near Clear Lake on our way home and disposed of all unwanted trash after a very long hot day which took three hours and twenty minutes to drive each way.

Back at home I made the horrifying discovery. We had cleaned out my car of all its garbage, and had also accidently thrown away all the applications we had spent the entire day collecting in the miserable heat. I was completely devastated due to all the time and trouble we had gone to.

The good news is that after about six months, I actually fell in love with this little City called Ukiah; you couldn't have paid me enough money to move back to Redding as it was becoming much larger than I was comfortable with. I began making more friends with people from our church and elsewhere and kept looking for a place to call home, all the while living out of boxes.

Until The End

Under the starry sunset, the ocean waves aglow. A silent night I lie listening, hoping that you know.

I want you to know I love you and I never will forget. All the sweet boyish things you did as you grew up as a kid.

The best child a mom could ever have you never gave us trouble. You had your share of mischief but well worth it even double.

I can hear the waves crashing in by the ocean shore. I think about my baby boy down on the ocean floor.

Can you hear my thoughts of you? Can you feel my pain? Do you see the teardrops run down my cheeks like rain?

Or are you right beside me, knowing all I do, one step ahead in every thought, as I think of you.

Do you ever speak aloud to me and wonder why I don't hear you. Or do you stand in front of me just hoping I'll somehow see you?

Or are we both in different worlds, separated by the veil, not for always and forever, but just until I get there.

Oh what a glorious meeting that day will surely be, no longer a boy but all grown up, a man you'll surely be.

I know that day will truly come only if I do what is right, and listen to the Holy Ghost morning, noon, and night.

Now it's getting breezy, the wind is feeling cold. It's time for me to leave you here but not forever as you know.

I miss you and I still am sad you had to go away. But my trust in Heavenly Father grows deeper every day.

For I know he'll bring me back to you in the twinkling of an eye. I'll try my best to be happy, and try so not to cry.

Our parting is just temporary and only for a while. Soon I'll see your handsome face, upon it a huge smile.

I thank the Lord for knowledge that we'll be together again, so until that moment comes, I'll love you till the end.

The Pain

I still feel the pain each time I see a photograph of you. For in the farthest back of my mind I just know this can't be true.

So I wait to get a call from you, a text or Facebook message. Trying hard not to let myself believe I'll never get them.

Your life on earth too short was lived, I held you just yesterday. That little blonde boy with curly hair who I knew would always stay.

You couldn't leave us we were not done, our time on earth together. With still so much for all to do, with your sister and your bothers.

We never thought you'd be leaving us, not the way you did. My broken heart still bleeds for you when I think of all you could have been.

But you're gone now and just a memory with photographs to share. A love inside a Mother's heart so deep and in despair.

I still try not to notice that you really went away. I wait for a call, a text, or a Facebook message every day.

I often feel you with me on the darkest days I have, and I know you're still here somewhere just not on this earth to be found.

I hope that Heaven knows what a special angel they behold. For in my arms just yesterday I had you here to hold.

I still can feel me pushing you in the baby swing. The hours we'd spend together. The way you loved to sing.

I pictured you a grown man someday with children of your own. I still keep checking for that message or text on my phone.

Oh how can this be really real when you were just here yesterday? I hear your voice, your laugh, your cry, you couldn't have gone away.

The only thing I can think of that even makes sense to me, is that God took you to Heaven, and that Heaven is here with me.

I don't think you are far away, not far away at all. Just on the other side of the veil, waiting for me to call.

I know you're right beside me although I cannot see. For God took you to Heaven, but Heaven is here with me.

Facebook Post:
September 15, 2011

"is Riding a Black Unicorn Down the Side of an Erupting Volcano While Drinking from a Chalice Filled With the Laughter of Small Children"

Finally a Miracle

Someone from the cute apartment complex, which was low income and that I wanted to move into, called. They left a message on my answering machine while we had been to Disneyland with my mom. It was received just twenty-eight days after I was told there was a two year wait.

What a blessing. I was so excited! It was a wonderful place to live and we finally unpacked and called it home. After a short time of being settled in our new home I began making more friends, Kate, who I had just met, along with my best guy friend, Eddie. He was awesome. We did everything together. He was my absolute best friend. Then that awkward moment when we decided to actually date. I met his parents who were in town visiting, as his sister and her kids also lived in Ukiah. We then went to a Chinese Restaurant for dinner and I don't think there were ever two more uncomfortable people on a date before. So, from there we decided to just remain best friends, and we still went out to eat, but it was just different being best friends vs. dating.

Best friends I could handle. He was tall, dark, and handsome but a cowboy; hat, boots and all. I just wasn't into that. It's too bad because he was a very nice guy. And of course, Grace and Jamie, who I am still friends with today, and many more.

Ukiah is a close knit community and people are like family, very close. Grace and I were great friends and went to a lot of the single adult activities together. That is where I met Norm and she met her husband-to-be, Dave, who she is still happily married to. When they met, Grace had two of the most darling little girls from a previous marriage, about the same ages as mine, and a handsome son as well.

I also had a very good friend, Stacy. We were getting married just days apart. She had a little boy and her ex lived somewhere in Texas, where she was from. She hadn't grown to love Ukiah as I and most others do. In fact, she had a nicknamed it, "yukyuk". Just three days before her wedding, coming home from work in Hopland, she was hit head-on by a 77-year-old man who was trying to commit suicide. He was unharmed. She was pronounced dead on impact. Her son ended up having to go live with his dad in Texas, and our wedding day literally went like this: got married, went to Stacy's celebration of life, and then off to our honeymoon. Not at all what I had expected.

Five years of being single from my previous divorce, I met and married Norman Crawford who was to become BJ's dad.

Facebook Post:
October 15, 2011

"As I do the laundry, wash the dishes and take out the trash, I wonder: Will Benderella get to dance with the princess charming at the ball?"

This saddens me deeply. I had no idea when I allowed the boys to stay with their dad just how much responsibility would be dumped on BJ's shoulders. He had to do so very much at such a young age. This is when I feel like I abandoned him and it fills my soul with such guilt ☹.

Another World

When the pains too much to bear, where then can I run to? I close my eyes you take my hand and bring me there with you.

Together in another world not so far away; within the twinkling of an eye we were both there yesterday.

The place we lived with God above before we came to earth, where we promised to be faithful before our mortal birth.

Yet once born all forgotten so challenges we bore, not knowing our way back to Him we had to learn once more.

Our faith we had to learn again and in Him to rely. I open my eyes and you're gone again, I just lay back and I cry.

For I know the true meaning of His plan and why He sent us here. It doesn't stop the hurt inside nor does it stop the fear.

I know angels are all around me even though I see them not. And a glorious world awaits me in a land that I forgot.

But when I close my eyes again you briefly take me there, I get a glimpse of eternity of which will help me bear.

All things that I must go through, though very hard they seem, one day I'll wake up in that world with you and it won't all be a dream.

Facebook Post:
October 18, 2011

"That feeling when you're texting four people, but none of them are the person you want to talk to"

The Family Begins to Sprout

Funny thing is, as we often dated and would go to the Oakland Temple where we would worship, we both knew beyond a shadow of a doubt we were going to have two more kids. I had the name Michael picked out ever since I was an eleven-year-old. Our neighbors had a son named Michael and I've liked the name ever since. Kelli I had picked out six years before she was born and it's funny how I would write about her in my journal and my mom and Norm and I would talk about her all the time. We definitely knew she was coming.

Norm lived in Santa Rosa, California, about an hour and twenty minutes' drive south of Ukiah. We'd both commute to date as we'd met at a church dance and had become quite the couple from the beginning. Even though I dislike dancing, in the singles groups there is not a whole lot more they offer and not many ways to meet new people and I did want to marry again someday and have more children. So, since I already had two daughters and he had one, we decided on having two more. We knew we'd be having Michael and Kelli.

Michael and BJ were both delivered at Ukiah Valley Medical Center by Dr. Mariano. They say Italian men are God's gift to women. I don't know about that, as my first husband was Italian, but Dr. Marino was certainly as close as it gets.

There is a certain swagger about Italian men that strikes the right balance between arrogant and insecure, manly and boyish, and, best of all, sexy and silly. An Italian man's face tells his life story. When it comes to Italian men, its good looks, style, guts, sense of humor, appetite, and arrogance. Let's face it, young or old, Italian men are simply sexy.

Having a very cute doctor was a bit uncomfortable at first but I got used to his charm quickly. He had a warmth and sincere care and concern for women. Now this was a man to be desired. He was always telling jokes, always had a smile on his face, was always in a good mood, and was always very professional when it came to his work.

Unfortunately, we miscalculated Michael's due date and he was delivered about one week too early. He ended up with Respiratory Distress Syndrome and had his head in a bucket with tubes all over the place and was in ICU. I'd just had a C-section so I could not walk or get out of bed to even get wheeled into ICU to see him. It was so hard having a baby and not being able to even see him. However, his dad stayed with him every moment.

The doctors kept saying he was getting worse, not better. I would get so upset, and they'd tell me he'd be in the hospital at least another ten days. My doctor wrote a note allowing me to stay a fourth day instead of going home on the third day following a C-Section. I remember crying and my nurse, who was also a friend from church, kept reminding me of the blessings God gives us and reminded me to be patient, stay positive, and not to get discouraged. I had a hard time with that as doctors kept saying he wasn't improving. Once I was finally able to see him and nurse him on his third day of life he began to get better and actually ended up going home with me on day four and has been strong and healthy ever since. Another miracle!

So we had Michael and were content to know Kelli would be next. I eventually became pregnant and knew it was Kelli. Why? Because I felt God had personally given me revelation telling me I would have a boy named Michael and a girl named Kelli…so I KNEW! I had an ultra sound and it said I was going to have a boy. I told everyone it was wrong because "I KNEW" I was going to have a girl and disregarded it as being an error. I was shocked when BJ was born…also C-section, as were all six of my children, though I had one miscarriage before I had Michael.

Anyway, I decided I'd better choose a boy's name for him as this certainly wasn't Kelli. I was dumbfounded and didn't understand why my Heavenly Father would tell me I was having a girl named Kelli and then give me a boy. I started to even doubt my faith. It never occurred to me until much later that I had more children coming.

Like I said, Norm and I had my two girls, ages 6 and 9 and his, age 5. We had only planned on two more, but sometimes God has other plans we don't know about. So BJ was born December 15, 1995 though Kelli wasn't born until years later, Aug. 15, 1998. With all my girls I had gained approximately 40 pounds and had lost the weight on each. With all my boys I'd gained around 50 pounds, still lost it, but it was a bit harder each time.

BJ was the biggest of them all. He weighed in at 9 pounds 14 oz. He was almost a 10 pound baby. He got his blue eyes from me, only his were bluer than blue; crystal clear like the ocean waters. As it turns out, his birthstone is blue topaz which matches the color of his eyes and is also the gem stone for the state of Texas where he was to later die.

We moved from California in 1996 as their dad was a roofer. We did great, except for in the winter when it rained, which really set us back. We struggled financially and ended up having to file for bankruptcy as we had no alternative. We had been living off credit cards when there was no work and I at the time was a full-time stay-at-home mom and didn't work nor did I want to.

I loved being a stay home mom and am not one who felt trapped or deprived. I like getting to spend time with my children. I figured I didn't have my kids so that someone else could raise them. I wanted to be there for all their "firsts".

Norm actually moved to Salt Lake City, Utah after securing a job. Once he got there, the guy had changed his mind, so he gave him $500 cash and left him to find another job. He was living in a small travel trailer. Back then we did not have the internet or cell phones so I would get a phone call maybe once a week as it was all we could afford.

Moving to Salt Lake City and living there for three months turned out to be a good thing. He found a house and sent me videos so I could see what it looked like on the inside as well as on the outside. Still, it's always so very different in person. He secured an even better job with a roofing company that is still around today and has since spread out to other states and is doing very well.

Facebook Post:
October 25, 2011

"Oh my god, I actually had a good day!"

The one's that make me so sad, and make me wonder…

1st Mother's Day

I was determined to make this day be sad with you no longer here. Until my dear husband who you said you liked made it full of cheer.

He bought me flowers that made me smile and a letter that did say, he knew you still loved me very much and would not want me feeling this way.

Plus other children I do have and they all need me too, and maybe even more now because of the death of you.

So I pulled myself together and my outlook I did change. I knew you'd want me happy on this day and every day.

I went to church, I smiled, I laughed and thought of you with joy; deep in my heart wherever you are you're still my baby boy.

Death cannot take you away from me I'm your Mother just the same. I'll love you for all eternity and smile when I hear your name.

For I truly know you are happier now and in a better place. We must both move on our separate ways until united by His grace.

Sometimes I feel you watching over me and know you love me still. So when someone tells me to have a "Happy Mother's Day", you can count on it, I will.

A Special Note:

"Dear Mom, I love you, And I hope you know you are the Best Mom ever. And I'm so lucky to be you're son. And I hope you live a good life. I think you'll be happy after you finish this letter. Love:B.J,"

BJ was about ten-years-old when he wrote this. I have this laminated as a bookmark and can't get it copied to the right size with his original little handwriting but here is what it says…a note he just left for me one day.

The Big Move to Utah

In 1996, Norm, myself and our five kids all packed up.

Just before we moved away from Ukiah to Salt Lake City, Utah, my mom took us to the beach. BJ's first time ever. He loved it! I have video of him doing some kind of, "Look at me everyone, I have legs!" I held him up and he would squat up and down and up and down again and again. It looked adorably funny.

BJ was just 9-months-old when we arrived in Salt Lake City, Utah. I remember he did this weird thing that my husband called the "Military Crawl." He would crawl with his arms flat on the ground. He once was stung on each arm by a wasp and I felt so bad. Poor little guy just started crying like crazy and we had no clue what had happened to him until we finally found the dead wasps on the ground and the two sting marks, one in each arm. I'm not sure he ever crawled normally but he was unique in many ways.

Benjamin got his name BJ due to it beginning with a B and having a J in the middle because his older brother could not say his name correctly. On his

Christmas stocking we noticed the B in the beginning and J in the middle so we came up with BJ for a nick name and it stuck like super glue. He's been BJ ever since. In high school he chose to be called Ben, due to the fact kids can be so cruel with their teasing.

So, I started out with Michael and BJ…not knowing until later I was supposed to have more children as I had set my goal at two more. All six of my children were planned, once I knew I was having them, and all six of my children were C-sections. The first two I bottle fed as I was still smoking, and I breast fed the remainder. BJ was the one I nursed the longest. People, especially his dad, kept telling me it was time to wean him off, as he nursed well over two years.

I loved the way our four-level home was built. Whoever built it, built in a food storage room down in the basement along with a family room with a pellet burning stove which was to become my oldest daughter's bedroom. I loved how the shelving had a slant and the cans or jars of food would roll down as you took one out, always putting the newest in from the back as you filled it. I had it crammed full of baby food. Every single flavor and brand, everything that was currently available; and at that time there was quite a lot. (I will never understand how all my children were so good to eat their vegetables as a small baby yet once they started on solid foods things changed. Almost none of them liked them anymore until they got past the age of 12, after which I began adding them into their diets again).

At Toy's-R-Us there was some kind of Pokémon card trading thing going on at one point and

I believe that was BJ's first exposure to Pokémon. He later lived it till the end. His dad even took him to Indiana once with a friend for a Pokémon Tournament. Scott, who also went, tells of some memories he has of BJ and the Pokémon tournaments and Indiana later in this book. He knew all the characters and would collect all the cards. Pikachu Chu was his favorite, I believe. I know he once dressed up like Pikachu for Halloween. He had a stuffed Pikachu he kept and slept with as if it were alive. I tell ya, sometimes I'd wonder. The tail came off once and he asked me to sew it back on. I noticed the stuffing inside of it was bright red. How very odd. It reminded me of blood, like it was alive. He finally passed the creature down to Nick when he got a Pikachu about ten times bigger. Nick now takes care of Pikachu as if he were real. It has his own bed, a pillow, and is always tucked in and covered up at night.

Facebook Post:
November 4, 2011

"Death Note and oreos... Come at me lonely weekend, I'm ready."

BJ, 2 weeks before turning 4

When Dinosaurs Ruled

I did in-home day care and BJ loved all the babies and would always be so gentle with them as he played. Michael was always with BJ, glowing with pride. You could tell from his little dimpled cheeks just how much love he had for his little brother. They were inseparable. Each time I would go to Ream's down the street on Fridays the boys were allowed to pick out a new toy. Nothing expensive, just from the cheap toy section. That was when BJ discovered his first love for dinosaurs. He'd get a new one every single week. He knew their names, what kind they were and all about them and studied them in depth at such a young age. He had big ones, medium sized ones, small ones. He had just about every kind of dinosaur known to man. We once took them all to the Dinosaur Museum at Thanksgiving Point. He loved those dinosaurs and stored them all in a large laundry basket.

One day, just for kicks, I decided to count them. He had over 200 dinosaurs in that basket. Even though some of them were quite small, others were quite large. Any way you looked at it, that was a lot of toy dinosaurs. BJ knew each dinosaur individually by name. He also had a large collection of stuffed animals that must have come to life at night when we weren't looking. They were his friends, quite literally.

One year, when we lived in Texas, and during New Year's Eve, we were watching the ball drop on TV. BJ's dad had already gone to bed so it was just me and the kids. He was watching the count-down get closer and closer.

Wait!!" he yelled suddenly, running upstairs. We had no idea what he was doing as we had a downstairs restroom, so that wasn't it. Moments later he came down, arms full and clutching tight to his many fuzzy, furry friends; his stuffed animals. He quickly lined them up on the couch and just in time.

"Happy New Year"!!! he sang.

Events like this would always excite him. Every year he'd open the front door, yell to everyone and shut it again. We'd throw confetti or balloons; nothing major. It would last a few minutes, be over with, and he'd be finished, more than ready to go to bed, feeling exhausted and proud for having stayed up until midnight.

Time went on in Utah. We thought about possibly expanding our family. We finally prayed about it, if and when we were supposed to have another baby. And so we had Kelli, finally, with her oh-so-round little pumpkin face, always smiling. We had already been talking about her for 6 years. It was if she was already born and a part of our family. We anticipated the day of her arrival. So, as the days got closer I decided it was time to explain it to Michael and BJ. Michael must have been easy because I honestly don't remember. BJ on the other hand…I thought he'd be very happy when I told him he'd no longer be a baby boy, but would now be a big brother. Boy, was I wrong. He just cried and cried and cried….then he told me, "I want to be your baby boy forever". So, ever since then it has always been a thing between us up until the day he died. Almost every time we talked I told him he'd always be my baby boy forever.

One day we were in Smith's shopping. Nothing kept me homebound. I would take with me whatever kids weren't in school. I would have them each hold a section of the cart and go shopping. People would look at me like I was nuts with all these little kids tagging along.

They were all so well behaved, too. I must add that bribery really works and 50 cent donuts, fresh from the bakery, was a small price to pay to keep them that way.

Anyway, as we were going through the frozen food section, BJ put his hand through the freezer door and got it got stuck. I tried to open the door further but the movement seemed to squish his hand even more.

I tried closing it a bit and to my horror it only seemed to tighten down on his now bruised and swollen hand even more. By this time we had attracted a small crowd and people were feeling so sorry for him. He was crying. Ladies were opening boxes of popsicles and giving them to him and the other children. Someone had gotten the store manager and some other workers who tried to pull on the door to open it wide enough to release his fingers.

Nothing!! By this time, as with all my pregnancies, I was fine when I stayed moving. It was usually in the grocery store line that this happened. I would begin to feel sick, like I was going to pass out, throw up, or both, would feel covered in sweat briefly, and would have to sit down and drink water or something...so it happened this time as well. (I later found out the sudden sickness had something to do with my blood circulation, etc). So, a man ended up holding BJ as I sat down in a chair, very pregnant, with Kelli in the baby seat. I was drinking water so I wouldn't pass out., so worried I was about my little guy.

Nothing anyone did was doing any good. I pictured his fingers majorly squished and broken once we got them out. Finally, the store manager called the fire department. I was so relieved to see them, yet so frustrated that they, too, didn't seem to know what to do.

By now I was becoming frantic. It was taking way too long. BJ was crying. No amount of ice cream or popsicles would make him stop. We were encircled by numerous people, all watching as this event unfolded. And then, you could pretty much hear a sigh of relief in unison...they removed the freezer door. At last, his squished, flattened, little bruised, but unbroken fingers were free and I was one relieved mommy.

Of all people, you'd think praying would have been the first thing to cross my mind. Fortunately, there is a song sung in church that reminds me, but no, I didn't think to pray that day. In fact, it never even crossed my mind - once.

An old lady in the checkout line later told me she had been praying for him. Where was I? That Smith's is not far down the street from where I live today, about the same distance, only from the opposite direction.

I could never go into that store after that although I used to shop there all the time, (even when BJ was alive, when he and Michael had chosen to live with their dad after the divorce). There were just too many memories inside of that store. Even after BJ died, it took awhile to return to it, but finally one night I did, I walked in. Everything seemed to be where I had left it like it was just yesterday. Even the Toaster Strudels and popsicles were in the same place.

I remember walking down that isle just standing there…remembering that day. An emptiness filled my soul which made me leave the store before bursting into tears unexpectedly like a firework going off in the sky.

Facebook Post:
November 2, 2011

"I feel as if the value of the every-day human life has decreased significantly. Most of the people you know and love right now will never amount to be anything worthwhile, and will never contribute anything to society. Their death would affect you greatly, but that's only because you knew them, who they were. Society doesn't care who they were. To society, their death is just another hair on life's ugly head.

And let's say you do amount to something, you DO become successful. No matter what it's for, there will always be someone more qualified, smarter, stronger, better looking, there will always be someone better than you. And there's nothing you can do about it, because that's life, and life sucks."

I Thought We Were Finished Having Children :)

There I was, thirty-five years old, 5 kids of my own, all C-sections and not planning on having any more. At a follow up with my doctor I asked..."So, we aren't planning on having anymore kids, but…what if we change our minds down the road, what are our chances?"

He said, "You're thirty-five years old, you have five children. I think you should be content and call it quits. I really think to have any more you would really be tempting fate. Unless you feel inspired to do otherwise."

Although we weren't planning on having any more, those words and the thought of never being able to have another baby made me cry all the way home. I was just so sad. I talked to my husband about it and neither of us wanted more…at that time.

However, as time went by we each prayed about it and felt there was one more little spirit up there meant to be a part of our family and even though I knew it would be quite risky, I knew it was a risk I had to take.

Kelli and Nick were both born here in Utah at LDS Hospital, delivered by Dr. Duran. He was, I later found out, one of the best doctors… and the best looking, I might add, at the hospital. He had just returned from a tour in Washington where he had given a seminar. He had also written numerous articles in the New York Times regarding his expertise. Kelli's doctor had since retired so I was left to find another doctor.

Living in the Salt Lake area and doing day care I only knew how to get to a few places at that time so I preferred staying close to home. I chose a mid-wife who worked at the same building as Kelli's retired doctor. When I discovered they didn't do C-sections, I was referred to a Perinatologist. I was terrified. I called a nurse friend of mine asking if they were any good. She assured me they were the "best of the best". In fact, that is how I initially got in contact with Dr. Duran.

The doctor was Spanish. He had an intense magnetism, with green eyes rather than dark as most other Spanish men, making him irresistibly gorgeous. He also had long eyelashes and wavy dark hair. He carried his bronzed body with great pride making one wonder if that meant he had time to travel and vacation on beaches, or if he merely had the natural dark sun-kissed look that Spanish men are famous for.

The nurse told me that they specialized in high risk pregnancies and emergency C-Sections. Although I was neither, I feel now that had we had any other doctor, we probably would not be here today. What normally would have been a 30 minute start to finish procedure turned into 90 minutes. I had a spinal this time instead of an epidural and it started to wear off and the poor anesthesiologist didn't know what to do so he put Ketamine in my IV…I later told my doctor I felt like I'd been on a 'trip.' He told me I probably had as the drug was related to LSD.

I remember everyone wearing hats. Then they all looked Chinese, then it seemed like I was looking through a kaleidoscope with the colors all changing and I remember asking over and over again, "Am I dead?"

The young twenty-two year old anesthesiologist felt awful. My doctor told me later, "I didn't want to say this with your husband in the room, but that was one of the most difficult C-sections I have ever done!" So, me and the baby, both, were lucky to be alive. And so our little family began.

As BJ grew he came to love the snow. Literally!

No matter where we were going, whether to the store, to church, a friend's house or whatever, I'd be getting the kids all piled into the van and inevitably BJ would run from the side door, from under our carport where the van was parked, off into the front yard area. He would grab a huge handful of snow and shove it in his mouth. There was no way of stopping him. It was like watching a starving kid who suddenly saw food and ran to not only enjoy it, but to survive. He just had to have his snow. We finally stopped asking him to stop and get in the van and allowed him to get his lifesaving mouthful of snow before leaving the house before heading off somewhere, as this became his ritual. Michael made a great friend, and to this day has a toy, of sorts, that he gave him so many years ago. They loved when it snowed.

Since I did daycare and church music was my focus, for several years I never listened to the radio. Boy, was I missing out. When driving around, the songs that would go through my head were either church songs (which are OK for Sunday, but not every day) or Teletubbies, Dora the Explorer, Mr. Roger's Neighborhood, or a few other kid shows. (Thank goodness my mind later chose to block them out so as I can no longer remember them. There were just sooo many and that's all we'd watch all day long).

One year for Christmas I bought each of the kids a Teletubby. Kelli's was red, Michael's was purple, BJ's was green, and Nick's was yellow. For years to come, the color yellow was Nick's signature color. Whenever he was asked to choose a color that's what he'd pick because that is the color he associated with being HIS color.

My children also had the Sippy cups and bowls, but since they didn't have purple, Michael's became blue, BJ's was still green, Kelli's was red and Nick's was yellow. That is, until we found out BJ liked green better, and Michael liked blue, and of course Kelli liked pink and purple. So they grabbed on to their own identity and chose their own favorite colors which changed along the way as they grew. Nicholas loved yellow for many years to come but finally let it go and moved on to red and then blue. BJ's last favorite, unless it had changed again without me knowing, was orange.

BJ's finger incident was actually the first real injury the kids ever had. I have a weak stomach and if the kids lose a tooth I want to pass out. I was also overly protective. A famous talk show host once said a parent can't be too protective because all it takes is that split second of them being out of your sight and they can be gone forever.

I once went to K-Mart (which is now sitting vacant) there to buy the boys long sleeve shirts and pajamas for them all as well as for my nephew, Kenny. Kelli thought she was being cute hiding inside the middle of a clothing rack which scared the crap out of me. I probably chewed her out bad enough so that she never did it again.

But I am sure I hindered the boys' growth. My now ex worked all day and was tired when he got home and didn't feel like going outside and chasing them down the street to catch them if they fell on their bikes, so I did what I could when I was big and pregnant.

He took them over to the church parking lot once. They had been gone so long that I pushed Kelli over in the stroller. I found him asleep and the boys not really knowing what they were doing, as they were not used to being outside of our yard. (The bushes started just about the middle of our front yard and around the corner to the side as we lived on the corner. That was as far as they were allowed to go alone).

I tell ya, I still believe you can never be too overly protective. Ever. Even when your children grow up. Having one of them kidnapped was the greatest fear I had.

The children loved playing outside. Their dad had built them an awesome fort, a tarp from roofing scraps with a ladder going up into it and a slide to come down. It had two swings on the side and a baby swing. I would spend hours and hours pushing BJ in the swing outside. He loved it. There was also a sandbox, and as BJ grew, he too was able to enjoy all that there was to offer. The baby swing was bought for Michael in California, then shared by BJ as Michael outgrew it.

Michael was so incredibly smart at such a young age. And so, one day, Norm got him a computer. He said in the future he'd need it for school, etc. I always thought it was pointless and unnecessary. Then, I finally let go of the intimidation factor, became willing to learn, and must have asked Michael 101 times, "OK, now show me just one more time, how do you turn the computer on?" Back then we would turn it off and on between each use. Little did I know that what I once thought was pointless would one day serve as a means for my job and the ability for me to work and be able to do so from home.

After about five years we then moved from West Valley City, Utah, to Broken Arrow, Oklahoma. Norm had lost his job, just when we'd gotten the house exactly as we wanted it; new inside paint, new windows, new vinyl fence, new roof, new walls, new carpet, and a new A/C-Heating system.

The U-Haul broke down before we even made it out of Salt Lake. They'd supposedly fixed it. Then there were times we were going 20 miles an hour while everyone else was going 70. It was pretty scary. We finally found a rest stop and called for help. The U-Haul was finally fixed after being stranded for five hours with five kids and a box of Honeycomb cereal.

We finally made our way to our new home in Oklahoma. Ahhh, our first real experience with humidity...and the buzzing sound from the trees. They bother you at first, and then you get used to it. Just like our home in Salt Lake City, the airplanes would fly directly over our house, one after another after another. We'd sit in the front yard the first few nights in amazement until the noise just became a part of everyday life. However, I would often go into the boys' room and watch...watch the headlights of a plane to come in, seconds later, another, then another, then another, just as straight in a row as could be. I would find comfort knowing our house was seventy-six years old and still standing when we bought it. So the odds of one of those planes crashing into it was pretty nil...

Text - 2012

I just read this quote on the internet: A man who treats his woman like a princess is proof that he was born and raised in the arms of a queen. I love you mom.;)

Life in Oklahoma

We moved into a lovely home which was a "lease to own" option. The owners, Norm's boss and his wife, had done a good deal of remodeling. The kitchen had been totally redone and the cabinets, with lighting inside, shown through the glass doors. There were lights everywhere in that kitchen. So much so, not only did we not need nearly so many but it would have cost a fortune to run them all the time, so we took out every other bulb. It was still the second brightest room in the house depending on the day.

Another room had been added onto the house. It had one wall with a door; the rest was entirely glass with sliding doors along with three large skylights in the roof. They called it the sunroom. We absolutely loved that room.

The first night in our new home we all slept on the floor. It wasn't until rainy season we began to notice something rather disgusting. Somehow, somewhere, worms, big, thick, fat, long ones would find their way inside our home and then somewhere about half way along the carpet they would die and dry up. I couldn't count all the dead worms I picked up from the carpet with paper towels. Somehow the plush carpet didn't seem so appealing anymore, as far as lying on it, or even sitting on it for that matter.

This was the year BJ started kindergarten. I still had that, "Have to keep an eye on my kids every split second, mentality."

There was just one house next to ours and then Vandever Elementary School. I would often be out in our back yard and look over and see the window to his classroom and wonder what he was doing. A lot of parents are happy when their children are finally off to school. Not me. I missed them terribly and couldn't wait until it was time for them to return home from school, show me all the many things they had made, tell me about their day, and how much home work they had, etc. I would go in front of our house to wait for him and if it took what I perceived to be a bit too long, I'd start walking over to the school to get him, always that fear of someone taking my child away.

I did daycare here as well. Only, by now, my husband was making a bit more money so I was able to get by with just one full time little girl not much older than Kelli. They got along rather well so it worked out great and her mom and I became like sisters.

We were allowed to put in an above ground pool, thinking one day we'd buy the house anyway. We soon found both the good and the bad in that decision.

In our backyard, we had gophers and they started digging up holes everywhere, all over the lawn. My biggest fear was that they would somehow dig a hole into the swimming pool so luckily we got rid of them before that happened. The good: we had bunnies in our yard every single day. What a blessing! They were so adorable and fun to watch and it simply amazed me that we could actually go outside almost any time of day to find bunnies hopping around.

(I remember once in high school when I was just seventeen. I took the Greyhound bus from Redding, California to San Rafael where my best friend and her husband had moved to. Then, as I was coming home, crossing what is called California Street from the Lady Lorenz Hotel where you catch the bus, back over to what used to be the Cascade Theater, I had that moment of déjà vu'. I had dreamed that very dream before. I dreamed I was walking across the street at just that very spot carrying my suitcases).

Well, it happened about 3 months after we moved to Broken Arrow, Oklahoma. My husband was sitting in the car waiting for me as I ran into the bread store to buy a few items. We'd saved so much money that way, especially on treats for the kids. I was in line when all of a sudden the blueberry muffins, everything around me was just as it had been, exactly, in a dream I had had about three months previously. Another déjà vu' moment. They are hard to explain if you've never experienced one, but very weird even still when you have them. It's like pre-knowing something you can't possibly know in advance, then reliving that very moment all over again. Kind of like what happened here.

Norm sat in the car while I ran into the bread store. All of a sudden it hit me, just as it did when I was seventeen-years-old crossing the street. I had been here before, in this store, in this lane, looking at this very package of blueberry muffins that someone else had put on the counter, but abandoned. I had been here before, but how? How could I know every detail I was seeing as this particular bread store was not the usual one we shopped at? In fact, we had never been here before, or had I? How else could I explain knowing something before I knew it?

Although we were only in this City of Broken Arrow one year, a lot of big things happened. George W. Bush was elected President. 9/11 hit. To this day on Facebook people still ask, "Where were you?" I was at the nearby Albertson's with my little day care girl, Chantell, along with Kelli, and Nick. The other kids were in school. It was early in the morning and I overheard the guy in front of me talking to the checker about the World Trade Center. At first, I didn't think too much about it, it was just casual conversation, then I got to wondering why they were talking as if it had just now happened instead of years earlier. I started asking questions and learned something new was going on. I went home, and like most of America, spent the rest of the day glued to my TV set in utter disbelief.

For days afterward, the school sign in front of Vandever Elementary read, "Bless America." When I first saw that my heart sunk. How could this be? How could we leave God out of our lives at a time when we needed Him most? It was so sad to drive by and look at the sign every day.

(I understood the schools changing things like "Winter Break" instead of "Christmas", as I had grown up as a Jehovah's Witness from birth to age 10. We were few and outnumbered at our school. We were made fun of a lot. We were not allowed to salute the flag and on days when they had a "Christmas" party or any other holiday party we were unable to attend).

I remember so clearly the day I drove by and saw they had added the word God; now it read, "God Bless America!" Boy, did my spirit soar as I'm sure many others did as well. I'm assuming enough parents had complained and so the school gave in and put God back in the school where He belonged.

That was also a sad year for those living in the city of Houston. That was the year Andrea Yates drowned her five children in the bathtub. My heart broke for those children, the oldest being just two weeks different in age from Michael who was seven.

I also learned that when it comes to snow, people in Oklahoma do not go out in it, LOL. Poor Michael. When he turned 8, we had to make a few phone calls to get people to come to his baptism even though there was only a few inches of snow. And here we'd been used to kids going to school with eighteen inches of snow. Seven inches was nothing and church activities were still held without power. In Oklahoma, just a sprinkling and everyone freaks out and no one wants to drive in it. But, I do have to give them credit. They are probably smart as they do have some pretty bad ice storms which can cause the roads to be very hazardous.

And of course it was also the year of our dearly beloved Shrek. The first children's movie I had fallen in love with since Lion King. BJ was the kind of kid who not only liked to make others laugh, but thoroughly enjoyed doing so. He loved being the comedian, the center of attention, the funny guy on stage everyone laughed at. He'd do almost anything to brighten your day with a good laugh. I still have a video of him, I'll need to have transferred to a CD or something, but he's singing the song, "I like big butts and I cannot lie." And getting so into it with his dance moves it is absolutely hilarious!

This was also the year my brother and my nephew Kenny came and stayed with us. Kenny was eleven and in the fifth grade. He was an awesome kid, full of energy. The job promised to my brother wasn't nearly what is was supposed to be, things didn't quite work out and after just six weeks they moved to Tulsa, then back to California. They had actually come from Texas where my dad had been living before he died at the age of 60 on September 11. 1999.

Ever since I'd quit smoking in 1987 I'd taken up walking…but the exercise wasn't quite cutting it anymore. I felt I needed more and this was the beginning of my introduction into the world of jogging. Kenny would go with me at night and I tell ya, he'd never get tired. He'd always keep up and could probably run circles around me as we went. They didn't stay long enough and I didn't like to go alone at night. It was too hot and humid during the day and my treadmill wasn't made for jogging so I put it off till another time, a time in the future when it became a part of me.

BJ's youngest brother, Nicholas, had just started to say a handful of words, was potty trained, and seemed to be progressing at the average rate as his siblings had. I took Kelli to the Tulsa Health Department for her kindergarten shots. Nick had had a shot at 9-months-old and they gave him another one at fifteen-months-old. They gave him his kindergarten shot that he wasn't supposed to have for years to come. They admitted it was an accident but said it wouldn't hurt him. So, we watched as he stopped talking, and slowly regressed. All we had taught him unraveled and became undone, unlearned.

We refused to accept the fact he could be autistic. It took years to finally accept it. During this time he developed some odd habits. He didn't speak again until he was four. He would drag his box of toys to the top of the stairs, and one by one by one sit and watch them fall, roll, slide, or however they would go down the stairs. He would watch so intensely, so precisely and accurately as if to figure out exactly how things were taking place.

Nick also would build what we referred to as his "Crop Circles." He would take his Pull-Ups and place them in order starting in the center then going around in a circle over and over making it as big as he could, hence, crop circles like many of you may have seen on TV. He still wore Pull-Ups but only at night.

He also had strange eating habits. If he had cheese puffs with his lunch, he would bite off the end of one, put it down, grab another, bite off the end, then another…until he got to the other end and would proceed to do the same things with the other end of each cheese puff, and then eat the center. The puzzling thing was, when he was finished there would always be remaining, one entire untouched cheese puff left on his plate. It happened every time.

Both BJ and Nick loved swimming in the above ground pool we had out back. The kids would swim just about every day. BJ had also found himself a girlfriend his kindergarten year. He had the same girlfriend his entire year and only split up with her because we moved away to Houston after living in Oklahoma for one year. BJ was true to those he cared about and committed to the end. If he was your friend, he wasn't your friend just for a few weeks, months, or years. He was your friend for life. He had long commitments to relationships and was loyal till the end.

The company my husband had been working for, who owned our house, was in financial trouble. They kept asking him if we were going to buy the house. Norm figured, although we had our doubts and concerns with all the many things we'd found wrong with it (now we had discovered carpenter ants!) that we'd go ahead and buy it. We thought if the boss's company did well, Norm's job would be safe. So, the boss, knowing full well of the kind of situation he was putting our family in, fired Norm one month after signing the papers.

Facebook Post:

"No, but your comment made me realize that I should have either said "I'd be Buddhist" or "it' be Buddisms", meaning that I was grammatically incorrect and am in shame. I am sorry English Language, I have finally failed you on the internet."

In Transition

So, once again off on another venture to find work, only this time landing a job in Eufaula, Alabama. Not a place I would happily choose but he found a job and jobs were getting harder to come by. The house was beautiful, the one we had picked out. It had, I believe, eleven fireplaces. Very large, spacious and affordable. The only problem, (if you want to look at it as a problem) was that my children would be the only white kids in a predominately black neighborhood and school. The lady selling the house was white and told us the natives were very friendly.

As I accepted this place to become our new home (even had a welcome packet sent to us in the mail), big changes occurred, something may have opened up in Houston. My husband said, "We'll never move to Houston." I told him he was wrong, I believed it was a possibility and told him we were going to move there. I put all of my positive energy and hopes into moving to Houston.

My husband did find a job there and was in a hotel for three months as the kids and I were at the house in Oklahoma trying to get it to sell. (The same thing occurred when he came out to Salt Lake City, Utah, and we were left in Ukiah three months trying to sell our house). We finally did a lease option and luckily after a year the people bought our home in California.

With my husband in Texas I had a huge yard to maintain and mow. Front, side and back, as well as keeping up on the pool. Some friends once brought noodles (pool toys) over that had been in the lake waters and we got mustard algae. It was so hard to get rid of, not to mention expensive, but I finally was able to do it.

I looked at the aerial map last night and it's now green along with one other pool in the neighborhood. (Eerily, the entire time we lived here, BJ had been living between New Orleans and Houston Streets with Galveston just beyond…how very coincidental, and just strange!) They built a deck to the pool and looks like they enclosed the glass side of the house with siding; I couldn't get a view of the rest.

So Norm would come home every other weekend only. I pretty much lived the life of a married, yet single mom. He had a good job and we had a house being built in Atascacita. We found it just as cheap to build a new one as it was to buy used. The time came for us to be out of the Oklahoma house and we drove to Texas.

The Atascasita house was not quite ready, and after our family had been living in a hotel for nine days they told us it would be another three weeks. So, we started looking around for houses that were ready to move in NOW! We found one in Porter, Texas. Between the two we'd drive back and forth.

Though the one in Porter was ready to move into, we called it the "Plain Jane House," as it was not nearly as fancy as the other one in Atascasita. That one was amazing. Norm had picked out all the colors, the cabinets, countertops, carpet, flooring, everything. But three more weeks in a hotel???

Interestingly enough, as we drove back and forth looking at each house trying to decide which one we wanted, I saw it. It wasn't another house, but a drive through store I had dreamed about approximately six months earlier. I remember telling Norm I'd had a crazy dream about this store; you could just drive through and I drove through it and bought milk. Well, there it was, looking like a red barn and all with all the neon colored lights at night, exactly how I dreamed it. This was not one of those déjà vu moments, but an actual dream I had talked about after having had it. So, with that, I made him drive through it. I wasn't sure if there were others that existed or where, but never in my wildest dreams had I imagined this store could be real.

The food there was expensive, and we did go there on occasion to buy a few things now and then. Needless to say, this was the final straw that broke the decision of which house we were supposed to move into. Plus, every single day, anywhere I went, I had to drive past it in order to go anywhere as it was between our new home and everything else.

Facebook Post:
November 8, 2011

"IF I were to choose a religion, it'd be Buddhist."
http://zenhabits.net/zen-attachment/

So Began Our Days in Texas

We began unpacking the over-packed U Haul and all of our worldly possessions. The kids were frantic with excitement. Driving for hours and being in a hotel room for days, they now had room to run, and run they did. Up and down and all around that three story house. The third floor was a huge room which we used as the kids play room and later as my exercise room as well. It also had a huge walk-in closet where we stored a lot of things.

Unfortunately, I learned that pictures don't store well in the heat and neither do dress shoes for church. As I unpacked my personal clothing the vinyl material on my church shoes had literally melted off just sitting in a U-Haul for those 9 days while we were in the hotel room. Also, our cans and cans of food storage made out okay, but storing them in the garage was not such a good idea. It definitely shortened their shelf life.

All in all, we had plenty of room for anything and everything we had, and then some. The house was huge and amazingly beautiful even though it didn't have the granite counter tops, the spiral staircase, and all the fancy things the other house had. We were just grateful to have a place to call home. Plus, it was in Montgomery County vs. Harris County so our property taxes would be much lower.

There was a sitting room as you walked in, with a couch and a computer. This room eventually became enclosed with double French doors to become my husband's at-home office. Across from it was the dining room. Then a half bath, the kitchen and a large living room area with lots and lots of windows. The view outside was stunning. We were in a spot that did not require us to put up a fence and so we never did. There were large pine and oak trees just beyond the grassy back yard, followed by a walking trail that circled the entire subdivision and each and every cul-de-sac therein. The boys would literally tell us they were going to play in the forest which, in fact, they did. We lived close to Kingwood, another city which was nicknamed "The Livable Forest."

Back to the house. I think there were maybe seven steps, then a landing, then a turn going up then another seven steps with a huge window where the landing was. If you walked straight you would be in what became Michael's and BJ's room while my second oldest was still living at home.

Once she graduated and moved away, Michael took her room and Nick and BJ became roommates. Nick and Kelli shared a room for a short time until she moved out, giving both Michael and Kelli their own rooms. BJ and Nick became best buddies. BJ was officially Nick's interpreter. Nick had a little language of his own that no one else could understand except for BJ. We had put Nick in pre-K at age four, and when he went to kindergarten, his teacher suggested we let him repeat it as boys mature more slowly than girls, and the fact that he was diagnosed with high functioning autism. Other than social skills with peers, he was a brilliantly smart kid.

(Looking back, I somewhat regret holding him back a year as he is so above most kids his age; not only in maturity but in height. He towers over me at age fourteen and I am 5'6". He's beginning to grow a mustache already, too!)

Nicholas began to speak when he was four-years-old. But until then, I remember for three weeks straight, he'd only eat cottage cheese about 5-7 times a day and absolutely nothing else. After that three week period he never touched it again, until after he was 12-years-old…and even then, rarely. He would just point to things he wanted, and when he'd be requesting something else and try to talk to us, we could never figure out just what in the world he was trying to say so we'd get BJ and he'd get it right away and let us know exactly what it was Nick was asking for or wanting. BJ was very protective of his little brother Nick and they played together well.

Facebook Post:
November 9, 2011

"I sat on the toilet sideways today
Fight the power"

Surviving the Hurricanes

I remember the year Hurricane Rita hit. It was September 18, 2005. Norm was brave but I had never experienced anything like this. Growing up in Southern California until age ten and then moving to Northern California, I knew my earthquakes. I remember being a little girl standing in the hallway in 1969 getting ready for school and a quake hit so hard our little fish bowl got knocked over. I remember all the earthquake drills at school. But hurricanes! That was new to me.

Hurricane Rita whipped through our neighborhood not doing too much damage. A roof off a car detailer had blown off and a few other minor things, but nothing major. A neighbor had boarded their windows and spray painted, "Rita Blows".

BJ was with me on this one. He and I found what I believed to be the safest place in our three story house. It was the laundry room off the kitchen with the half bath on the other side. Open the door and the entry way to our home had two large windows. The living room was full of windows so I could imagine glass blowing everywhere as we only had one side window boarded on the upper landing of the stairway going up. We sat in there for hours listening to the radio, singing songs, having visits off and on from his siblings, who, by the way, all thought we were over reacting. We finally got bored out of our minds and figured if we died it would be better than living in that laundry room forever although there had been no complaints on space as it was huge. We had no power for several hours. Just a battery operated radio, a flashlight and candles. It was quite cozy.

Rita made landfall as a category three landing. In the aftermath of Hurricane Katrina, Hurricane Rita triggered one of the largest evacuations in US history. Hurricane Rita was responsible for 120 deaths. Some were actually associated evacuation efforts, such as the twenty-three passengers who died in a bus accident south of Dallas, Texas. Total damages resulting from Hurricane Rita resulted in over $10.5 billion (2005 USD) making it the ninth costliest hurricane to affect the United States.

Then Hurricane Ike blew in on September 13, 2008. Ike was headed right towards downtown Houston and was going to be huge. I had gone and done some shopping at Wal-Mart Supercenter where they had everything you could imagine. I never valued wet wipes so much in my life until this experience.

A bit later I learned a set of missionaries were going to be staying with us as they were being evacuated from Pearland, Texas. Their apartment had gotten flooded, so they, along with many other elders, needed a place to stay. I figured we had plenty of food but decided to go back and get some "snack" food just to have a bit more variety on hand.

I was shocked when I arrived at the very Wal-Mart I had just previously been to. The shelves were literally bare. Last minute panic had taken over the small city of Porter, Texas. There was absolutely no bread whatsoever left on the shelves. Just a few remaining bags of tortillas, which I grabbed, just in case. All perishable items were completely gone. There was absolutely nothing left. Canned goods and other supplies, even frozen foods were all pretty scarce. The price of gas rose to an all time high, and pumps everywhere were turning up empty. Gas stations were being forced to close down as they had no more fuel. Now this was scaring me.

So it was Norm, me, Michael, Nick, BJ, my other son Damien, their best friend, Kelli and the two missionaries all huddled together. We listened to a radio once we lost power. I couldn't believe what I was hearing. By now it had hit downtown Houston and they were talking about full offices, furniture and all, chairs, desks, computer's etc. flying out of high rise office buildings. Could this really be happening? Was I going to wake up and find it was all a dream? Or, were we all going to die?

We all went to bed not knowing if we'd again see the light of day. Then early in the morning we woke up to an eerie, shrill sound. We were in the eye of the hurricane. It was freaky scary. I was looking out of our bedroom window on the second floor of our home and began taking videos. The tall, fifty foot pine trees (filled in with oak trees) were swaying heavily.

One of them on the side of the house that we had kept meaning to have someone cut down, I was sure would land us. Then it got silent. It got eerily calm. We had been stuck in the house for four days now. No electricity or water by the time everything was over. The electricity we could have done without a bit longer I think but this was where the sanitary disinfectant wipes came in extremely handy. I was able to clean countertops, etc. prepare food, clean up after we ate, and keep the bathrooms as clean as possible without water.

The kids got a bit too excited as our cul-de-sac tended to flood and all the kids in the neighborhood were out in the puddles of water, playing in it. I hesitantly let my kids be kids and get dirty with the rest of them only to later regret it. I had no way to bathe them. Their wet clothes they had changed out of began to smell, and very badly.

I grabbed my camera, took my daughter, and we went driving around our subdivision. I was blown away, (not literally) but just about everything I saw was. Fifty foot trees had been uprooted and their roots were taller than most cars. Fences were down all over the neighborhood. Trees had fallen over blocking roads into and out from our subdivision. People were mean and had absolutely no patience for others, especially those taking pictures. If you were in their way you'd better move, NOW!

Back home we learned the silence was merely the calm before the storm. The real hurricane hadn't quite hit us. So we huddled in our house listening to the sound of wind ferociously blowing, howling as it was just outside our door and windows. Were we going to make it?

The wind seemed to go on forever. Unless you've ever been smack dab in the middle of the eye of a hurricane it's hard to explain what it's like. Creepy, eerily scary, just weird, and different than anything you've ever experienced before. Finally it calmed once again. It had passed, it was over, and we had made it with absolutely no damage to our house whatsoever. The rest of the neighborhood and all around the city didn't have it as good, however. I remember it taking months and months to finally get everything cleaned up.

We had milk cartons filled with drinking water, and an 1/8 teaspoon of bleach added to keep it pure. It wasn't the best but it was all we had. Soon we heard the coast guard was meeting in several locations handing out bottled water. I remember I never thought bottled water tasted so good. I was not one to buy bottled water as I saw it a waste of money when you could just turn on your faucet and get it for free, but this was heaven. It was especially good as the days got warmer and the weather more humid and muggy. The bottled water just tasted so much better than what we had stored in our milk cartons so we used that water to wash some dishes and things.

The Coast Guard was very generous in amounts they would give out as well; it depended how many people you had in your family. I remember driving to the location. Everyone was in a line and they would ask, "How many people?" You'd tell them and open your trunk or the back of your car and they'd load you up.

My husband took me out for a drive, camera still in hand, because I wanted to see the full devastation all around us. It was pretty much the same everywhere. Trees brown over on top of cars, houses, buildings with roof damage, lots, and lots, of uprooted trees. We took some videos, and my son Michael helped put them together in a way that made them look cool. We then posted them on YouTube and I believe they are still there if you Google Hurricane Ike, Porter Texas part 1, part 2, and part 3.

Everyone was finding baby squirrels that had fallen from the trees and taking care of them for weeks. One by one they all died. A worker, I believe from Kansas (where else?) was there as one of the many helpers. He was working on the power lines and was electrocuted. One of the videos is in memory of him.

We tried keeping the kids as clean as possible. We collected rain water in what we had been using as a toy box. One by one we had everyone wash their hair and I'd rinse them off using the rain water. After four days with no power and no water, (though our neighbors had a generator) we were told it would be another two weeks at least before everything was back to normal.

At that point we took Damien to his grandpa's and headed to Corpus Cristi as most people had headed the other way. The missionaries stayed with two other missionaries at our bishop's house. They at least had running water. Our house was considered by FEMA unlivable and they actually ended up paying for our hotel room. We didn't know they were going to at the time.

We drove past downtown Houston and saw the devastation we had heard about first hand. It was like watching a horror movie, or a sci-fi; it was surreal. Rooms were much cheaper here, and we had a Radisson Hotel by Marriott which was very cozy. It was a two-room with an adjacent door so the kids had their own room. After we arrived there and got things unpacked in our room I did two things:

First, all of the kids had a nice long shower and got very clean. Second, I grabbed all the laundry and we found a Laundromat. Everything smelled like it was moldy even after washing it. The smell remained even after washing it multiple times but the smells eventually went away. The sad part was that our neighbors called after two days, once we had bought enough food to last two weeks, and had a kitchen and all, and said the power was back on. We didn't want to go back home. We were having fun, it was our vacation! My work at the call center was even excusing those in Ike's path.

Ike peaked as a Category 4 over the waters of the Atlantic. Hurricane Ike was the third costliest of any Atlantic hurricane, killing 195 people, 74 of which were in Haiti, 112 in the US with 23 still missing. It hit Cuba on September 8th. The hurricane weakened prior to continuing on into the Gulf of Mexico. It gained strength until a final landfall on Galveston Texas on September 13th. Damages from the coastal inland area alone were $29.5 Billion with additional $7.3 Billion in Cuba. $200 Million in the Bahamas, and $500 Million in the Turks and Caicos amounting to a total of at least $37.5 Billion in damages. But we survived!

Facebook Post:
November 19, 2011

"Got my own room: YES!"
"Friends comin over: YES!"
"This party's rockin: YES!"

God Took Your Light Away

Standing in the water you are all I feel. I know you're out there somewhere you made the ocean real.

I know I'll always think of you every time I see a piece of driftwood on the sand a shell or just the sea.

You're everything about it no matter where I go on this land. Not the mountains or the trees just the ocean and the sand.

I write your name upon the shore the waves wash it away a memory all too clear that you have gone away.

The lighthouse is still burning bright for the entire world to see but the light inside my baby boy God took away from me.

All I have now is this spot and memories of you. The laughter of a lifetime of a baby boy I once knew.

JUST DON'T FORGET ME

You grew into a handsome young man making your mother so proud. But the ocean is now where you live the waves are now your shroud.

I know you still live on somewhere inside this watery grave. You'll always be my hero for you were so very brave.

You lived your life with dignity to make other people laugh. To cheer them up when they were sad to help make them not feel so bad.

You had a heart of gold and to all others you would give. I'm not sure why your Father took you now and you no longer live.

You'll always be a part of me I never will forget, my 4th. child and my 2nd son I never will regret.

I miss the times together that we could spend alone. Or me helping you with your alphabetical order a homework which made you moan.

The times alone at Subway with just the two of us; or Sonic for a quick bite until you've had enough.

You and your friends I loved dear that played through the neighborhood down at the bridge at the pond fishing with your gear.

For Cumberland seems empty now since you're no longer there but Galveston seems livelier I know your spirits there.

I'm Not Alone

Among the waves the moonbeams flicker as if dancing across the ocean. The tide is still for a moment, while the hurricane approaches.

Safely snuggled under the sea, I'm warm and unafraid. I have no regrets you chose for me this shipwreck watery grave.

Those above about to die as the hurricane approaches. Once again a tragedy, but each one leaves them choices.

They move away but some rebuild and do it all again. For those who die come live with me and wonder why they did.

If knowingly time and time again the same thing seems to happen, why do so many deny that fact and try to start all over?

If living in the same old place could mean their life is over: do they think, do they dare, do they even care?

The waters getting choppy now the moonbeams flicker gone. No more dancing upon the waters, now it's just a song.

First every melody plays out so swiftly and abrupt. Then suddenly without notice the hurricane's upon us.

Screeching, wailing, Shrills, of sailors ghosts gone by. A hundred sounds of children crying as they slowly die.

These are just the sounds we hear of the hurricane alone, and not yet to touch a home. But they all knew it was coming, most have gone away. Soon we'll have more company with those who've chosen to stay.

The ocean is a beautiful thing but God hath no control. The evil one hath power, to take away man's soul. We cannot live upon the earth without the evil and the good. What seems to be so harmless is immensely misunderstood.

So now it is upon them, for those who chose to stay. Some did survive, however, but many died that day. Why must we think we are so great that we will never die? It's all a bunch of garbage, it's from Satan. It's a lie.

So now you all are with me and under this mass we'll stay. While demons do surround us Our God will never stray.

Each year our clan gets bigger. If only eye could see. There are thousand's down here with me in the place you buried me.

*Facebook Post:
December 10, 2011*

"life has finally turned around"

School Days

One morning BJ and his friend Reece were waiting for the school bus to pick them up. It was pitch black in the mornings when they'd catch the bus. BJ came running into my room, me sound asleep, him yelling, "Mom, mom, we just saw a UFO." He then went on to describe what he had seen. He was serious as could be, scared to death, shaking, the whole bit.

I finally convinced him it would be okay, to go back out and wait for the bus. I wasn't sure what had gone on that day but others from his school had reported seeing the so called "UFO's" that morning also. Just one of those strange happenings you can't explain, but he wasn't alone. Lots of other kids had seen it too.

Reece, BJ's partner in crime, was a great kid. I'd take them to scouts and he'd always say, "Okay play it!" (ha-ha)…because he knew I knew what he meant. He knew that I'd have it ready and was probably the only crazy mom who would play Gwen Stefani's "*The Sweet Escape*," full blast driving down the street while they'd rock out. Especially Reece, (ha-ha). Gotta love that kid. It had to be his favorite song and I don't think he had access to it other than when he heard it on the radio. They'd get wild in the back seat of the Tahoe, rockin' out.

Back then I liked Nickelback. BJ absolutely could not stand the sound of Nickelback's voice. He'd say, "He sounds like he's constipated!" It took a year or so but eventually I guess they came out with a song BJ liked and he began to like their music.

Apparently BJ and Reece liked to play in the woods. They also liked to play with matches. Not a very good combo.

One day a girl saw them playing with matches behind her house and told on them. Apparently they got in trouble, however I was never informed. So, while BJ was spending the night with Reece, they decided to go egg her house. She lived in the middle of the cul-de-sac down from Reece. It was only five eggs. ONLY! Never underestimate the power of an egg.

A man appears at our door and says he was told our son and Reece egged his house but as he works out of town and has been gone a few days he has just discovered it. It had been very hot and humid.

We decided to get up extra early the next morning before church to clean it up. The people knew we were coming though they were not home at the time. There was a balcony on the top that you could either climb up, or get to from the inside of the house so the boys learned to climb. The boys, my husband and I, had a pre-mixed solution and spent hours and hours cleaning and scrubbing and finally got the stain off from the eggs. What a relief. We were a bit sweaty but nothing major. We even had time to hurry and get ready for church but I insisted we drive down their cul-de-sac just to view all of our hard work and efforts one last time.

What a saw made me sick to my stomach. I was horrified. The stains had come back just as soon as everything dried thoroughly. I couldn't believe my eyes. Poor BJ felt worse than ever, it was all over his face. I did some investigating and found a man who swore he could power wash it, so we split the cost with Reece's family. We paid him $100 and after he was finished I felt so much better and went to look.

"Oh no!!! Not again, they're back!" Those dang stinkin' egg stains just would not go away. I then talked to the owner of the home. He said he needed to get his house painted anyway so if we paid just for the front only...he'd pay for the rest. He got prices as well as us.

A good friend of mine, Nikki, who works at the tanning salon, had a brother-in-law who did the painting. Not only did he have the best price, he did an awesome job and it only cost us $350. We were at about $400 total and hours of hard labor for throwing five eggs to get back at a girl for telling.

Unfortunately, as I said, I was not informed earlier of the matches incident with the girl but remember the day BJ came running into the house in a panic telling me how he and Reece had started a forest fire, literally.

His jacket was soaking wet. I guess they were playing on the trails, making small fires and this one got out of hand so he panicked, got his jacket wet and tried to cover it over and over to put out the flames but the flames got too big for him and he came running home to tell me.

Luckily, a neighbor had seen it and called the fire department and by the time I walked over to where it was, they were putting it out. My thinking was, "No way is my kid getting off on this one. If anything, I want them to have a good talking with him."

So, I went home and got BJ and took him back over to where they had started the fire and told the fireman, "This is one of the boys who started the fire." I took him aside and asked if he'd at least talk to him. He was way too nice in my opinion but as far as I know, BJ never did it again.

I then drove over to Reece's house and told his dad, "See those fire trucks over there?" "Our sons are responsible for starting that fire." He looked dumbfounded. I believe his friend, Reece, also learned not to play with fire.

Still, BJ was one who liked to try things out; explore if you will.

He liked to go with his friends into the woods a lot. One place past the gate across from the school, rumor has it, used to be a very expensive country club-like place. The couple divorced and one of them burned it to the ground to keep the other from getting possession of it. There are roads that basically go nowhere. There was one that dips down and has water flowing towards it and I don't know a kid who's been there yet who hasn't been hurt. They call it the waterfall. It's very slimy and slick and if you're not super careful...

So, they passed beyond the waterfall, then to the other side of the school, still deep in the woods just walking around. They had gotten lost but were not afraid. They figured eventually they'd find their way, until they saw a large snake.

BJ called 911 telling them they were lost. Of course 911 wanted them to stay on the phone but his battery was low and so they hung up.

I get a call from the Montgomery County Sheriff's Office. "First of all, your son is okay," a woman says from the other end. They're not the right words to start a conversation and I'm thinking, which son? Michael? BJ???

The woman proceeded to tell me BJ and a friend had gotten lost in the forest and the sheriffs were searching for them and the best thing I could do was to stay home. (Also not a good way to be a conversationalist). So there I sat, or rather paced the floors back and forth.

That's when I found out from my husband that BJ's phone battery was very low. Panic, panic, and more panic. It was a comfort knowing the sheriff's office was out looking for them but not a comfort knowing they, he and another friend he'd rarely hung out with, had gotten lost in the forest with no way to contact them.

The sheriff's office decided to ping his phone signal to find the exact location. They did this several times until FINALLY...the lost boys were found. Oh, what relief!!! For a few months thereafter I referred to the two as Ping and Pong. Thank goodness for modern technology; it can often be used as a safety tool for a child.

You have to understand that BJ wasn't always your typical kid.

He was modest for a boy and didn't like just anyone watching him take a whiz. During gym class he'd always wait until one of the stalls was available so he'd have some privacy. On this particular day, however, he just had to had go. All the urinals were full as were the stalls. He couldn't hold it any longer so he went outside, around to the side of the building to relieve himself.

Coming back he got dressed into his regular clothes, when to his surprise, during his next class, he was called to the principal's office. Why? For going to the bathroom in front of an entire classroom full of kids.

He was devastated. He thought the darkened classroom had been empty. The school kicked him out for the remainder of the year.

I was burning hot and furious and went to speak with the principal who said, "Oh no, it's just 30 days in what they call TLC. It's an alternative school which doesn't stand for tender loving care. In fact I refer to it as the "Prison School."

Kids are not allowed to even speak to other students. EVER!!! Or they get points taken off. After so many points, they add more days and so it can go on forever if you're not careful. I still fought the 30 days asking what else he was supposed to do, only to be told, "Share a urinal with another student."

I'm sorry but at age 13, that's just not going to happen. Kids are teased enough. You don't just walk up to another kid using a urinal and start peeing beside him. You'd never live it down and the rest of your high school reputation would be ruined.

They finally agreed to cut the punishment down to 23 days. That was still not good enough for me. It was a sheer mistake and bad judgment on my son's part. He meant no harm and didn't know anyone else was watching or this whole thing would never have happened.

So, after going to a meeting with a few members of the school board and stating our case, the board cut it down to 13 days. I still was not happy but readily agreed when I was informed it could easily go the other way and they could press charges for BJ exposing himself. So, he did his time and came out none the worse for wear.

On BJ's thirteenth birthday, we had a big party for him. Unfortunately his birthday was on December 15th, so it often got overlooked as everyone was thinking of Christmas. Or people would combine his birthday with Christmas. I liked to make sure we kept them separate so he didn't feel cheated. He had it all planned out. Games they were going to play such as Pin the Tail on the Donkey, and several others along with a movie to watch and of course cake and pizza.

One of his friends had called at the last minute saying he could come but needed a ride. I didn't know where he lived, yet BJ's friend JT knew, so I took JT with me to get the pizza, and then to pick up this other kid.

They were currently doing construction on 1314 FM Road, making a one lane each way into a 2 lane each way street. It depended on the day, and which part of the road they were working on, what the speed limit would be. It could be 25 or 55 mph.

So here I was going 53 mph in a 25 mph zone. I got pulled over and the sheriff told me I was going 28 miles over the speed limit and asked me if I knew that. Me and my stupid answer. I told him it was my son's birthday and I had his friend in the car with me, that we were going to get the pizza and then pick up another friend.

I mentioned it was hard to keep track of the speed limit as they kept changing it depending on the driving area, and where they were currently working. The next big stupid thing I said was that I had another parent's child in my car while I was going 28 miles over the speed limit, and that I was on my way to pick up someone else's child as well. Smart me.

Luckily, he was in a good mood. He said another car had driven by his radar as I had gone by so he was giving me a ticket for 24 miles over the speed limit. Anything 25 miles or over keeps you from taking the defensive driver's training course online to get the ticket removed from your record, which is what I ended up doing. It still cost me over $100 but was worth it not to have that ticket showing.

I'd also gotten pulled over for speeding in Arizona. And the officer had said he was giving me an early wedding present, letting me off with a verbal warning since I had a clean record. My registration had expired and he never mentioned it; though to be honest, I hadn't been sure of the violation until I got to Utah. So, I guess it pays to tell the truth, even though had the complete truth been known he may not have let me off. I did get another speeding ticket in Utah for going 5 miles over the speed limit, so I'm thinking, "Seriously?" (ha-ha). But yeah, I just paid that one off and left it alone. I didn't mind a 5 mile over the speed limit ticket showing up on my records. Utah was also where I got my very first speeding ticket ever. I don't remember how fast I was going but it wasn't too fast. All I know is I was going more than 5 miles over the speed limit but less than 24. During my lifetime I must have gotten pulled over for speeding probably about a dozen times, but had only received 3 speeding tickets.

I'd received one in the state of Texas and two in Utah. So now when I'm on the roads I still tend to have a heavy foot but I'm more watchful, though truth be told, I do have a hard time keeping within the speed limits.

Facebook Post:
September 13, 2011

"Every highway's got its speed bumps...can't be goin TOO fast now"

Parting Ways

In 2009, Norm and I divorced. We had joint conservatorship and I had say of where the children lived. However, BJ and Michael both wanted to live with their dad. Kelli and Nick stayed with me. They don't normally split kids up, but allowed it under the circumstances.

He was the first to move out of our house and moved into a nice apartment complex with a pool, exercise room, etc. We stayed in the house a few months longer then moved into some low income apartments which were very nice. I loved the huge bedrooms and closets. We lived just five minutes away, so Norm would watch the kids for me when needed and it gave me a chance to see the older boys often.

Back then, not so much anymore, I had a thing about cleanliness. A lot of people called me a neat freak but after BJ's passing and due to health issues, I was no longer able to live up to my own standards of cleanliness which drives me batty so I just do the best I can and don't worry about it.

While I lived close to Norm and the boys, however, I would go over to their apartment every other weekend and clean the bathrooms. That would often lead to some cleaning in the kitchen as well. I figure, if anything, I wasn't going to have my boys living in a home with filthy bathrooms. Since I was always the one to do all the cleaning, they were never taught how and so I felt I needed to keep the bathrooms clean for them.

Before we divorced, we had already filed the paperwork. My apartment was picked out with my deposit on it and everything was set to go. Norm had a long airplane trip. It took forever before they were finally allowed to get off the plane. He's a big guy and those chairs aren't the best and so he developed a blood clot in his upper leg. I remember him being in pain. I took him to the ER where he sat five hours which was typical of this hospital. He wasn't even seen until then. He'd walked into the hospital, but due to waiting 5 hours, his leg and foot had ended up swelling and turning blue and purple, they had finally gotten him into a room, though nothing more had been done after that. Because his leg and foot had ended up swelling and turning blue and purple, killing a lot of nerves, it caused him to spend two months in the ICU.

The doctors ended up doing a fasciodomy to relieve the pressure from the swelling. His leg had swollen so much and the skin was so tight. He had some sort of vacuum machine hooked up to his leg which sucked the excess fluid from his leg. It was left open for two months, three slices down his leg, one on his thigh, and one on each side of his calf.

Once opened up like that, you can't just sew it back together, so they had to do a skin graft from his good leg. The poor thing looked like a patch work quilt with triangles, and rectangle shapes cut out here and there to cover the openings so they could heal.

When he was first released, they wanted to teach me how to change the packing in the wounds that needed to be changed on a daily basis. I refused, because I have such a weak stomach. We hired a nurse to come to our home every day to change the packing.

Our dining room was changed into a hospital room. We had a half bathroom downstairs just next to it but Norm couldn't walk for the longest time so I had to do everything for him. It's funny how you can be in the middle of divorcing someone you know you can no longer live with, yet still have compassion for them and care for them when something like this happens and no one else is around to help. So, that is what I did and I did it willingly, from sponge baths, to helping him brush his teeth, etc.

He eventually recovered. He could walk some but the foot being dead so long had left him with no feeling. He ended up with drop foot and is now permanently disabled and uses a wheelchair. That is mostly why I would go to clean, because the boys were never taught how, and Norm physically was unable. BJ ended up helping me a lot.

Once I was divorced I told everyone I knew that I was NOT getting into a relationship for at least a year. I might date if it came up but I wasn't going to be looking for anyone. If it happened, okay, but as far as a serious relationship, no way. This was going to be a year to be a better mom and to spend more time with my kids. To work on me and my relationship with my HP, who I choose to call God, and to improve myself. I've always liked the saying, "Stop trying to find the right person, but instead focus on being the right person, and then the right person will find you."

Facebook Post:
February 12, 2012

"... It's freezing. The air is frozen solid. We are walking through a solid mass."

Apparently God Had Other Plans

When Norm and I divorced in June of 2009, I was prompted to get on the Christian Singles site the following month, and there I met my current husband. He only had a few more weeks left of his six month membership. I had only signed up for three months.

I was very busy working that day from home for another call center. In between calls, and trying to pay some bills, the thought went through my head to Google *Christian Singles*. I KNEW it wasn't my thought, I also knew when the spirit told me to do something I'd better listen or lose out and no longer receive those promptings. If I acted on them and stayed in tune I received even more.

There I was, writing a quick blurb about myself in a hurry just to get the darn thing done so I could sign up for three months to see more than what you initially see when you log on. It looked interesting so I figured "Why not?"

Steve was one of the first ones I met. He was 45-years-old and had put 45 years and younger as someone he'd like to connect with. I was 46 and had put a few years older and a few years younger. Steve would never have seen my profile. I was the one to reach out to him first even though I'm 10 months older than he is.

It's sooo totally not this way in real life. I had so many guys wanting to email me, call me, message me etc. There got to be so dang many I'd forget who I said what to and it literally became overwhelming, so I decided this had to end. I needed to narrow it down and stick with maybe three and go from there.

Steve was always a favorite and I kept going back to him. He later told me it was his magnetic personality, ha-ha. I could have written a list of everything I ever could have wanted in a husband and checked off each one with Steve, in addition to qualities I would never have even thought of. He was all I ever could have asked for and so much more.

With all of that instant connection, we still broke up so to speak, if you can call it that. I was momentarily writing just one other guy. But I noticed something; when I'd get an email from him I didn't get those warm fuzzies I'd get when I'd see an email from Steve in my inbox. Also red flags went up a few times and I finally had to tell this other guy to go away and asked Steve if he was still interested in writing me. He almost said no.

We met in person in October. On that first date I picked him and his twelve-year-old daughter, Kelli, (same spelling as my Kelli) up at the airport, drove to my apartment where the babysitter and my daughter Kelli were waiting. Nick was at his dads. I dropped his daughter off, and drove to the Houston Temple for a session of worship; (we barely made it).

It was the last session of the day. I found out later that he was going to propose before we went in but we didn't have time so he'd decided to propose afterwards. We became engaged after our first face to face date, and then spent a few days together going to movies, to places for the kids, and then Steve and his daughter, Kelli, flew home.

I moved back to Utah in December, arrived on December 29, and we were married January 1, 2010. So much for no relationship within a year! I was married within seven months and was so very glad I listened and had Googled that website and found Steve or I may never have found him at all.

As for BJ, he and I did a lot of random things. Once I asked him to go for a bike ride on Christmas Eve.

He said, "But it's raining."

I said, "I don't care." We grabbed our jackets and left. In Houston most nights can be fairly nice weather wise; even when it's raining. I only recall a handful of days or nights when it was really, really cold but this particular Christmas had been a warmer one. We rode our bikes in the rain around the neighborhood and had a blast...who cares if the rest of our family members thought we were nuts.

I miss him. There are just so many things that come to mind when I think of him, from way back being a small baby, to a young boy, growing to an adolescent and a teenager, and eventually a young man who was greatly admired. He had a vision, just in some of the little things he'd say, almost as if he knew at times the end was near.

Before we moved out of our Porter, Texas house, I had a garage sale. I had so many winter clothes I had been lugging around for years, from Oklahoma to Houston that I never wore and figured I'd never be wearing again. I sold everything and never in a million years thought I would end up back in Utah; especially only about fifteen minutes away from the house we'd lived in when BJ was nine months to six-years-old.

It's really hard at times, as I pass daily, places I used to take the kids while growing up, places we would go when BJ was little. We still go to the theater where we saw "*Quest for Camelot*" and pass by The Old Spaghetti Factory and the K-Mart where Kelli hid between the clothes, which still remains empty, along with so many other places.

I'd planned on flying to Houston, Texas once a year and have the boys fly out to Utah once a year, but as it turned out, due to finances, they only came out once. That was BJ's last Thanksgiving. Eight months later he died.

BJ had been working out a lot and getting pretty buff. He wouldn't eat processed foods or drink soda. He was really taking care of his health. He was the tallest one in the family. He was even taller than his twenty-two month older brother.

Facebook Post:
March 5, 2012

"Who paid for this milk? Not me. I will never pay for no milk ever again. Not once, not never."

Shattered Life

I'm living now a shattered life that no one else can see. I wear a smile to mask the pain which lies inside of me.

My head is like a dam, just waiting to burst open. The tears I'm holding back now will soon be overflowing. My stomach has a hole inside it's missing you so bad. If asked just how I'm feeling, I'd tell you why I feel so very sad.

My heart is shattered into a million pieces lying on the floor. I want to pick them up but I can't take this anymore.

I feel hopeless and alone and I don't know how to go on. I sometimes wish my Father in Heaven would quickly call me home.

My life here is so empty, there's nothing for me to do. I live each day, each hour each minute, only missing you.

KIMBERLY A. CUTLER

That little boy He gave to me then took your soul away, I long to be there with you now, each and every day.

A Mother's child is not meant to die. My mind just cannot grasp it. For denial runs so deeply then depression follows after.

Why did he take a sweet child so smart and full of life? So handsome buff and caring, who would surely get a wife.

Your passion was the ocean with Marine Biology. Nothing in life now matter's, why could He not have taken me?

Those baby blue's I can't forget they match your birthstone well; Blue Topaz the gem stone of Texas the oceans blue tidal swell.

Laid to rest at Galveston Island an hour off the coast, after having your body cremated for cancer took the most.

I do not have a place to go to visit or say hello. So I hope the Lord gives you the chance to come visit me, I may or may never know.

To say good-bye just one last time might help me ease the pain. Until I see you smile again, I'll only see the rain.

I Held You By The Hand

2-9-2014
7 Months Ago

Seven months ago today I held you by the hand. Telling you it would be OK, I still don't understand.

Nothing could prepare me for what God was about to do. Take you back to your Heavenly Home and leave me without you.

I know now you are happy for you suffered way too long, but taking you away from us seemed oh so very wrong.

I trust the Lord with all my might and leave you in his care. I know that you are better off, up above somewhere.

Nothing could prepare me for what God was about to do. The days are long and lonely, and empty without you.

Your memory still lingers on with every breath I take. Every hour, every minute, every second I'm awake.

You are always on my mind and that is where you'll stay. Until the Lord comes to take me home and I see you again someday.

But until the day that happens, through this journey I'll endure. The pain, the grief, the suffering, unimaginable for sure.

No parent should ever outlive a child, that is not supposed to happen. The pain will never go away, life just continues on each day.

So if when I am smiling a tear streams down my cheek, you know who I'll be missing, I'm strong though I'm not weak.

I try to make the best of life but it will never be the same, not one thousand billion years could ease a Mother's pain.

No matter how much time goes by it still seems like yesterday. I held you by the hand telling you it would be OK.

8 Months Ago Today

Eight months ago today, I heard the angels call, they took you to your Heavenly home, there was nothing left for you here at all.

You knew I would feel lonely, you also knew I'd cry. But given all the reasons I'd also understand why.

Your job to do on earth was done yet no one else had a clue. But I knew you'd be leaving soon, I think that you knew, too.

The last few days looked hopeful. Our hopes for you were soaring. That night I flew home to Salt Lake, you died that very next morning.

How grateful I am to have spent with you the last week of your life. The time you seemed to be doing your best. Up walking and without strife.

Your doctor's all said you were doing well and should be going home soon. I'll never forget that moment I turned to get one last look of you in your room.

You cleared you're throat and said to me, "Good-Bye Mom, I love you." A pang then went throughout my soul I didn't know what to do.
I turned and headed toward my plane knowing I'd soon be missing you.

I got a call that next morning, you were sick and still in bed. They expected you to be leaving soon to your home in Heaven instead.

Your father let me talk to you though I don't know what I said. Oh what do you say to a son you so love who in minutes would soon be dead?

So the angels then came and took you home to the place where you belong. But I know I'll see you again someday when my time on earth is done.

But until the day comes that my time on earth is through, every hour every second, I'll be missing you! I love you BJ Crawford <3 Mom

A Grieving Mother's Heart

They say to "just get over it" but they don't understand. A mothers heart just doesn't heal since before the world began.

For God once gave you to me then he took your smile away. You'll always be a part of me each and every day.

At first I thought it would get easier as the days slowly went past. How little did I know the pain had barely come to pass?

With each day it gets harder while I try to carry on, mostly for your siblings or perhaps I too would be gone.

I need a reason to go on each and every day; just knowing you're no longer here is an indescribable price to pay.

I sleep to go into nothingness so I don't have to feel.
But I can only do that for awhile then I wake to face
what's real.

Those who have never been there will never
understand; a grieving Mother's heart will never be on
the mend.

For time does not heal the pain it only makes it
different. I scream I bet I crawl but I only find solace
on my knees when I listen.

For God so loved the world He gave his only begotten
Son, He loved you too so dearly and you've been a
chosen one.

You completed the test you came to do on earth your
time now gone. So into God's care He took you
home, your time on earth now done.

Soon enough time will be here to follow in your path
but not until I finish my work and do all that He did
ask.

In need to understand that my time is not here yet.
But one day soon it will all be over and in eternity
we'll bask.

Together again we both will be and all our loved
one's too, For God so loved His only begotten Son
and He also loved you and me.

Facebook Post:
February 9, 2012

"Lmfao again: its like eating soggy crunch" (talking about eating lettuce and tomato on burgers)

Feb. 2013 with Tyler Nathaniel Enloe
Galveston Fieldtrip

A Parent's Worst Nightmare

One day my ex husband called and said he was taking BJ to the ER. BJ had been throwing up, had had diarrhea for two weeks, and had lost ten pounds. He said he was now hyperventilating and complaining of back pain. The doctors checked his blood and urine and did an MRI and everything looked okay, so they said he had the flu and sent him home.

That was when my worrying began. BJ remained sick and at home the next two weeks. Because he wanted so badly to become a marine biologist, as a straight A student it was so important to him to go back to school and take the Taks Test.

The school arranged for another student to push him in a wheelchair from class to class in order for him to be able to take the test. This felt kind of silly to me. When you are feeling that sick you can't think straight to begin with but it's what he wanted. It turned out to be a blessing though.

His fever spiked and his blood pressure dropped so the school called my ex husband who said to meet him at the ER. This is the same hospital which had told him he'd had the flu, where my ex had sat for five hours to be seen.

They took BJ by ambulance to Texas Children's Hospital. While he was there, I was diagnosed (after 14 years of trying to figure out what was wrong with me) with "Mucus Membrane Pemphagoid (MMP)," a rare blistering autoimmune disease which only 3-5 people in a million are diagnosed with each year. One or two a year are diagnosed in the UK, less in places like New Zealand, etc. MMP is associated with T-Cell Lymphoma and mothers have a 25% chance of passing a gene down to their children.

Whether or not I passed the gene to my children, I don't know, but I can't blame myself or beat myself up over it. I believe everything happens for a reason in God's time and God had a higher purpose for my son to fulfill. He completed the work on this earth he was called to do and was needed elsewhere; it was his time to move on and nothing I could have done would have changed that.

On the day BJ was admitted I was on Facebook. I had liked the group *Kansas* as I have seen them in concert two times. Once they played with *Journey* as they opened for them in Redding at the Civic Auditorium in 1976. Their song "*Carry on My Wayward Son*" had always, always reminded me of my oldest son, Michael.

But for some reason, on this day it reminded me of BJ. I was a bit confused and stunned. Why BJ? That's the song that reminds me of Michael. Always has. It's never reminded me of BJ, so why now? So I Googled the lyrics. The part about "now your life's no longer empty, surely heaven waits for you," I had heard a million times but didn't know exactly what those words said. When I read them I knew. It just about knocked me over. I had heard the song so many times but never those lyrics....I knew then that BJ was going to die. Before he had a diagnosis, before anything, I just KNEW. I had received a personal revelation, one I almost wished I hadn't received, yet at the same time I felt I was being prepared for what was to come. I also found it ironic later, as I seldom listened to the entire two CD of songs, that at the very end of the last song they say "Thank you and Good Night from Texas!" So, apparently the CD was originally recorded live, somewhere in Texas.

As you recall, BJ found a girlfriend in Oklahoma and kept her all the way through kindergarten until we moved away from Broken Arrow. He then had the same girlfriend his entire first and second grade years in Texas. After that, there was one young lady in particular he never gave up on. He adored her. He'd buy her gifts at Christmastime only to have them returned. He tried and tried to get her to like him back, but I guess you can't always be lucky in love.

From what I know, his next big crush was in high school in Texas. I still have a small stuffed bear with a red bow around its neck he had given this girl for Christmas only to have his heart broken again and again. It sits on my computer desk here as I write, a reminder he'd had happy times and sad ones… but most of all a huge heart that had the capability to love others.

BJ was such a smart kid all the way around, but for some reason, writing in alphabetical order was just not his thing. It would take him hours to complete a page and he'd mess up and get frustrated, until one day I did his paper for him in about ten minutes. It was a breeze and I kind of liked it so I did his ABC order homework every day after that, for a couple of years. What was the homework really teaching him anyway? I thought. It's just making him frustrated, costing him so much time, etc.

He still got straight A's in high school, and in the long run, looking back, I still think I did the right thing (bad me) and would do it all over again! He tried his best at everything he did. I remember the school calling to verify if he had a live lion in his backyard. He also had a very vivid imagination.

He wrote Pokémon stories and drew pictures and had sooo many I finally had him weed them out a bit; something I now regret as I'd give anything to have something of his as I have so little.

He was very good and was accepted into a National Writer's Club. He had lots of talent, too. He loved to cook and bake so when he got to high school it didn't surprise me when he joined the Culinary Arts class. He used to swear one day he'd own his own restaurant and he already had the main ingredient...his secret sauce. It was awesome and everyone in the family loved it. It was a great dipping sauce for pizza, fries, corn dogs, you name it, and it was HIS! He was going to be the best. He'd make cakes and cookies more often than the older girls ever asked to. He loved being in the kitchen inventing and creating his wondrous treats. He also liked Aquatic Science.

There was a time or two he'd fight with his siblings and I had to put him in time out. One I remember oh so well, only because I was angry and yelled at him to not dare come out of his room until I said so. Hours and hours went by and life happened and all of a sudden I opened his door.

His quiet little voice asked, "Can I come out yet?"

I have never felt so bad. The poor little guy. I had simply forgotten all about him because he was being much too quiet. I simply forgot and got busy with other things that were going on.

My heart sank. I must have squeezed him and apologized a million times. I still feel bad to this day thinking about it.

Still, I feel so blessed that I was able to be a stay at home mom for so long. I was able to go on the kids' field trips. I remember BJ's 5th grade class going to the Houston Museum of Natural Science and Art. I hated the bus ride as it totaled my hair (ha-ha). But afterwards I got to know some of BJ's friends on a more intimate level than I had before.

The class made tie dyed T-shirts for everyone so we would not get lost from one another. On the back collar of mine it says, "BJ's Mom". Whoever was making the shirts didn't know my name. I still have the T-shirt, only now it is a very faded pale soft light blue color overall.

I have another shirt that was BJ's. It was originally handed down from Michael, who had gotten it from a neighbor. After the last visit there,

Nick had come home with some of BJ's clothes as they were so close in size. Nick is big for his age.

One shirt has always haunted me. I believe he had his 5th grade picture taken in it. It's a button up shirt made out of silky material, solid black with red, yellow and orange flames.

It is far too much of a reminder. To see him in the school picture wearing this shirt is almost more than I can bear. I tried to get it away from Nick to save it but Nick loved the shirt and wore it until he ripped a large area down the side which was not repairable. I washed it and gently tucked it away in one of my bottom drawers that I seldom use. I do occasionally open that drawer and see the shirt as a stark reminder and the deep pain and sorrow returns. I can visualize BJ wearing it in his class picture for 5th grade.

There were just too many things; too ironic as if all along God is just showing us the future. The shirt, the street names, the song, where they sang it even. I just needed to put it all together. I know, however, in reality they were merely coincidental, but for me, they remain as symbols of who BJ was, a stark reminder everywhere I go.

I see his face down every street I drive by, every Arctic Circle they used to play at, the Kearns Fitness Center where my husband has his night job cleaning pools - the same spot where Michael and BJ once took swimming lessons when they were little and we lived here before, the gym - where my son Nick trains with his coach, Bill. (I took Michael, Trish, and BJ there over Thanksgiving while they were here visiting and they met him). I often wonder why…why God brought me back to this exact location when there are so many other places I could have ended up. And my husband was here, so close to where we once were, the entire time.

Getting back to the fieldtrip...

The teachers paired each parent up with five kids so I had BJ, JT, Reece, Larry, and one other child I don't remember too well. But the others were good friends of his. One of his friend's parents had divorced so he lost contact with him which was sad because they were such great friends for many years.

Reece was his partner in crime for awhile. They'd hang out then stop, then hang out awhile. The other, JT, was always there, from a very young age and was one of the kids who went on the boat with us. I'll never forget that kid. When you have your kids friends around so much you end up learning to love them as your own, they just seem like family.

From the very first time I met JT, maybe when he was in the first or second grade, he was always so overly polite. He'd say things like, "You look very pretty today Mrs. Crawford!" I'd get such a kick out of how polite he was and had to keep reminding him my name was Kim. Still, he would flatter me off my feet every time I saw him. I can just imagine how he treated future girlfriends. He went from a scrawny little kid to a very nice looking young man.

Of course, there was another friend, Damien, who was both Michael and BJ's friend. They would fight every time he came over about who got to play with him. He remained a great friend to both Michael and BJ and was also one of the kids we took out on the boat, along with his sister Brittany and their parents. JT and Damien the other friend I would call my "other" son because they felt like sons to me. I'd hug them every time I saw them, even after I moved away and came back to visit once a year.

I still have this little two inch alien dude Michael, BJ and Damien won from the machines at CiCi's pizza. They named him but no one can remember its name. He's been sitting on top of my computer for more than five years now. A reminder of some of the good times we'd have, the way things used to be, but will never be again, even the lunch dates I'd take each kid on without the others knowing, making them feel special not knowing I did this for them all. BJ's favorite place was always Subway, if not there it was Sonic. Our mother-son dates will always be cherished.

I didn't tell anyone of my experience for about a week. It had to sink in, but it was true. I just knew it. So, finally I told my husband who listened with an open mind and understanding heart.

As the days and weeks went by and BJ got sicker, there were times my husband Steve would tell me he just knew BJ was going to be OK…that is what I wanted to believe and found great comfort in his words. At other times it would make me so mad because I felt I was told by God he would die so who was he to tell me otherwise? I already knew and nothing was going to change that.

My oldest son's girlfriend, Trisha, did a website for BJ and it can be found on Facebook @teambj. He's the 17-year-old kid wearing a baseball cap and a red shirt. She started this for me, along with a T-Shirt sale for donations to collect money to help me get back and forth to Houston as I went often during the time he was in the hospital. He was only in for about 2 months before he died, sick one month prior.

I'm so very thankful he was able to come on what would be his final Thanksgiving just before he got sick, and shortly before he died. Michael, BJ and Trish flew out and we had a pretty good time, however, I regret it never snowed while he was here. He wanted to come when it snowed. I also regret that we didn't just go drive up to the mountain snow, or go see the lights on Temple Square…all things reserved for another time. You never know when your last chance will be; you may not get another time.

Facebook Post:
March 10, 2012

BJ: Love you too! You need to see my fish tank! We should have all kinds of cool organisms by the time Kelli and Nick come to visit so it should be amazing!

BJ with older brother Michael, summer 2012

I was glad BJ had told me before he left, "You did good, Mom, you picked a really good guy. I like Steve." But I missed him.

When I'd talk to my ex he would tell me BJ was OK, and that if it ever got really bad he would call me and let me know, that it wasn't necessary for me to come out. I finally got smart and talked with his doctor and nurses and was told I had a very, very, very, sick boy. Very, (three times), is NOT good so I was on a plane to Houston the next day.

I took my two younger kids, Kelli and Nick, with me. We planned on staying a week. When I first saw BJ he was on life support. Two tubes were in his neck the size of my fingers, one going to his lungs and the another to his carotid artery. I could not approach his bed. He was very hard to look at, yet I wanted so badly to run over and hug him.

One of the nurses could see my hesitation and realized why and suggested I come around to the other side of the bed. Still, I could not get close enough to him as there were so many tubes all over him, just everywhere. IV's all over the place, monitoring every little movement he made. All I could do was run my finger through his hair. I'll never forget the feel of it, shorter than he used to wear it, yet soft and thick with a bit of a wave to it.

The noise from the breathing machine was so loud. To make matters worse, when BJ tried talking to me he struggled to get any words out and got frustrated. Then he reached for the picture paper board with letters and pictures on. He could barely use his hand...

Very slowly, with a shaky hand, he spelled out the word "text" by pointing to each letter.

His dad asked him, "So, you want to text your Mom?"

He shook his head, yes.

My ex-husband gave him his cell phone and he fumbled around with it a bit but couldn't do anything with it and got even more frustrated. Then he grabbed the picture sheet again and turning it over, finally pointed to a picture of a heart.

I asked him, "Are you trying to tell me you love me?"

He shook his head, yes, as a tear rolled down his face.

Just a day prior, his favorite teacher of all time had come to visit him and he was barely able to speak. He'd had her in 2nd and 4th grades. He told her she'd inspired him to be a marine biologist.

I had originally purchased my plane ticket and scheduled my PTO from work before he got sick. They were very good to work with me. The first trip out, I'd had my two younger children, Kelli who was fourteen, and Nick who was twelve, with me. The plan was to stay one week. The doctors and nurses took us aside and said I needed to stay. They said they rarely ask a parent visiting from out of town to stay longer, but felt I needed to, which meant they thought he was going to die soon.

I kept my younger kids with me one more week then had to send them back home to Salt Lake City as they were still in school. I ended up staying another week and a half. I went back I think two more times before my so-called planned vacation time.

And amazingly enough, this was the time he was at his best. He was off all life support machines and doing his physical therapy. We had long visits and good talks where I could actually understand him. Before, when he wore the oxygen mask, it made so much noise, even without it, I still had a very
hard time hearing, let alone understanding him. Plus, he was just too weak.

The first time seeing us on our last visit he'd gotten so emotional he'd started crying. The nurse asked if he was okay.

He told her, "This is my family from Utah."

Kelli and Nick were there for the summer. The nurse thought maybe it was a surprise but BJ was just so very happy to see us. Unfortunately, however, we'd learned that while putting the tubes in his neck, someone had nicked a nerve which had caused his right hand not to function properly. That frustrated him, as he had no idea what was going on.

We were told that in time, with physical therapy, he would get the control back. We also learned that at some point he had had a stroke as he ended up with drop foot. Still, we were told that in time, and with physical therapy, a full recovery could be expected.

Then the doctors had discovered a rather large blood clot. Luckily it was tied off and could go nowhere, but they'd found another in the other tube…free flowing, able to flow through his lungs up into his brain.

Now we were very worried.

. Everyone kept saying they were praying for him. I hated watching my son suffer so much. I started to just ask people to pray that God's will be done. God sees the whole picture. We don't. His ways are not our ways and we cannot comprehend the blessings He has in store for those who love Him.

When I first saw him, BJ's lungs had completely quit working. He wore a diaper which I'm sure completely humiliated him. He was on dialysis and his kidneys were failing. His spleen was enlarged and his white blood count was very low. He had horrible bruising all over his legs from hemorrhaging. All his internal organs were either weakening or failing and his heart was getting weaker every day. Still, with all of this, he slowly began to improve.

Little by little he began to be his old self again. The first words he spoke once the air tubes were out of his mouth and he was able to talk were "Icee…NOW!!!!" We took that as a very good sign! He always did love eating snow as a young child so it's not surprising Icee's were among his favorite.

Then BJ had a set-back. At one point the doctors realized he was aspirating a small portion of his food so they cut him off of food. They were supposed to put a port or something in his stomach so food would directly go there, but it was taking the doctors and nurses forever to decide what to do so he finally agreed to a Nasal Gastric feeding tube which would make him gag every few minutes.

He absolutely hated it so at 2 a.m. he demanded that it be taken out. They finally put some type of port into his belly button that went into his stomach which fed him. His words were, "I don't like it," and "it's not natural."

There were a lot of unpleasant parts to his hospital stay I won't go into because I really don't want to relive them again and repeating them doesn't do anyone any good, so...I will say this: I truly believe he had the cancer when he was here for Thanksgiving. It's a very fast growing cancer. I believe if they'd found out in the hospital sooner and had begun treating him for it sooner he would still be here today.

But I also believe everything happens for a reason and if it's not your time to go, you won't go and when it is...well, there's not a lot anyone can do about it. As I mentioned earlier, I feel God has a higher purpose for my son, a greater work for him to do than what he's accomplished on this earth and his work here was done. I just regret that the last three months of his life were in suffering and misery, yet he never complained, only about the feeding tube put down his nose.

Other than that, he fought a good fight till the end and remained strong for everyone. He's my inspiration and my hero. I sometimes whine and complain about the smallest of things, but my son was so very brave.

The last few days together were literally heaven, up until the very end.

One day BJ had overdone it a bit and said he was just exhausted and didn't want to do physical therapy that next day. We just figured it was because he had done so much the day before. The doctors were planning his "go home" date and calling him the Miracle Boy as he came back from the brinks of hell and was now thriving.

The next day was my last. I packed my bags into my rental car, checked out of my hotel room and headed for the hospital until it was time to head back to the airport. I got there and was a bit surprised he was wearing the oxygen again. Supposedly he was still okay, just very tired. We had the best day ever together!

I finally had to leave and we said our good-byes. I didn't know when I'd return. I took one last look back. He cleared his throat and said, "Good-Bye Mom, I love you." A pang went through my soul and I didn't know what to do. I told him I loved him, too. I knew I would never see him alive on this earth again...but I had to keep moving.

At the airport I sat shivering. I saw a Houston hoodie and I bought one. I put it on, still chilled to the bone, with an indescribable emptiness and sadness weighing down my heart. I came home and unpacked that evening.

My ex called me that very next morning telling me the HLH Lymphoma had come back and they didn't expect him to make it through the day. HLH is very rare. Only one to two children, out of a million each year in the USA, (usually children much younger) have the condition.

I went numb. My ex called a bit later telling me he had had to tell BJ he had cancer...as if somehow he hadn't figured it out on his own by now. Then I was told he had only hours left. There was no way I could get there even if I wanted to. Then it was just a matter of minutes.

I talked to BJ's nurse who said he wasn't afraid. I'm sure they had him pretty doped up at this point so fear wouldn't even enter the equation. My ex held the phone up to his ear so that I could talk to him, say my final good-byes. I still have no idea what I even said.

What does a mother tell her dearly loved son who will be dying in just minutes? Are there even words? I do remember trying to stay positive, letting him know that my personal beliefs are that your body dies but your spirit lives on and that we'd meet again someday. He'd be free from the pain and the body that was holding him back. He'd be able to do all the things he wanted to…again.

Then, moments later, I got the call. He was gone. I broke…my baby boy forever…gone!!! My heart sank. Then the Kansas song went through my mind again. And the knowledge from heaven, given to me by God, I believe, to prepare me for his death. How blessed I was to spend the very last week of his life down to the very last day with him.

I was also glad I hadn't been there when he died. I would have freaked out and ended up in the mental ward. How grateful I am to have spent his very last Thanksgiving on this earth with him and his older brother Michael and Trisha. How blessed I was to be his mother for thirteen years.

Not that I'm not still his mother, but before moving away to Utah to re-marry I feel I missed out on so much. I feel a lot of guilt. I feel things were placed on his shoulders he was not ready to bear.

Several times and within a matter of weeks I went back and forth from Salt Lake to Houston. I give a big thanks to Trisha for setting up the teambj account on Facebook which made it possible for me to travel and not work and be by my son's side.

My ex, however, was with him 24/7. He did everything in the world that he could for him. But I could only do what I could do and must leave the rest in God's hands.

BJ's little sister, Kelli, and little brother, Nick, miss him most as they lived with him the longest. His older sisters from a previous marriage were grown and gone before BJ got very big. Michael, I am sure, misses him more than anything. They were brothers, and not only that, best friends.

It's taken Nick awhile to process it all. He has high functioning autism and never ever forgets anything and to see his brother that way will be the way he remembers him. It's too bad. Nick's processing pattern is a bit different than the average person's and I am hoping he understands it.

I tried talking with him about it one day and he told me things that blew me away. He talked about the stages of grief. I asked him how he knew all that, where he had learned it. He said, "From the internet, and also from talking to counselors at school." So, here I wanted to get him into counseling when he was already one step ahead of me, and making progress.

I am grateful BJ waited until I was home before he died. Norm had Michael bring his siblings to the hospital. The last visit to Houston the kids had stayed behind and I'd been called the very next morning after my return home. I'd had a good sleep and was ready for it; I was able to hold it together and not shatter into a gazillion pieces.

BJ's in a better place now, free from pain and the sorrows of this world. His cancer ravished body no longer binds him down. He can use his right hand, run, do anything he so desires...and he's got his hair back! What more could a handsome teenage boy ask for? He's now free to move and do as he pleases, with no restraints. And, most of all, he's happy. And he wants us to be happy as well and not to feel sorrow for him, but look forward to that day we'll meet again.

His brother Michael said BJ would always say, "We're all just stardust anyway," so whether you believe in God, a Higher Power, Buddha, or a Creator of the Universe, we're all just little specs of dust, creating a constellation amongst a galaxy in the universe, which is much more.

Each and every one of us is equally important and numbered and also intimately known by our loving Father in Heaven. If you truly understand death then it's not such a bad thing. It's all a part of life and everyone ever born has to experience it.

BJ's now happy and free. How can I be so selfish as to want him back in that body he suffered so badly in, when I know in my heart he is happy... far happier than I ever could imagine? I know he wouldn't want me to be sad for him. I take comfort knowing I'll see him again someday.

I have heard people say, regarding my older son Michael...I can't wait till the "old Michael" is back; something most people apparently don't understand. You never get over losing a loved one. Whether it be a parent, where they say you lose a part of your past; a sibling or spouse, where you lose a part of your present: or a child, in which you lose a part of your future. You never, ever just get over it.

I would liken it to sending a son or daughter off to war. So, now that they are gone a month, you miss them terribly. Does six months of being gone make you miss them less, or a year even less? Or does it make you miss them and want them back just that much more? There isn't a day that goes by, nor will there ever be, that I don't think of my BJ.

Mostly when I am alone in my car and play my Kansas CD, a double track, that's when I am most reminded of him and I just cry. Crying is a way to slowly heal my heart and my car is my safe place where I can be away from the world and cry with no interruptions and allow myself to feel my feelings, or grieve if you will, and let a part of it go. The horrible, indescribable, no-words-ever-made-for-it pain I carry inside of me.

When BJ had been gone nine months I went through a very dark period. I had thoughts of suicide, major depression, and slept until I just couldn't sleep any longer. I no longer felt I had a reason to get up and face this cruel world. God, as I understood Him, I had abandoned, as He had abandoned my son. Or so I thought. At this writing, it's been a little over sixteen months since my son died. I hate it when people say passed away. They died, plain and simple. I guess it's a way to show respect but why sugarcoat it and make it look less than what it really is?

I began writing a book for him as he requested not to be forgotten. I soon realized I would never have enough of a story, or stories to write an entire book, so I initially gave up. I wanted to honor his memory though, so I decided to write a book of poems as I went through my grieving process, as those come to me so easily. I can write one in a matter of minutes and it is also very therapeutic as I am able to express my feelings of grief and release it.

The poem on page 157 was written for Janie Budro, inspired by her son Tyler Lane Budro, "Get Over It". This is for all of those who think we have a time limit. Those who think we have a set amount of time to grieve our loss and be done. That simply isn't true. For several reasons actually. Everyone grieves in their own way. Also, everyone has their own time table for grief. It actually never ends but goes on eternally as long as we remain on this earth without those who have gone on before us. We don't start loving them any less. We don't stop thinking about them and wishing they were here.

BJ was just seventeen when he died in July of 2013. He would have turned eighteen that December and we celebrated with his favorite, a raspberry cheesecake. When I say "we", it was a Facebook, "Come Wherever You are" party. Buy some cheesecake and have a slice with us in memory of BJ's 18th Birthday.

Many of his teambj fans joined us that day from all across the US. We'll be celebrating his 19th birthday this Dec. 15th. I am so hoping to have this book done by then as a present to him. He's not gone. He's just on the other side of the veil. I can often feel him; hear his laughter in my mind, the funny things he'd say. Of all our kids, he was THE GOOD kid who never got into trouble at school. If a teacher came to us with a complaint and said it was BJ, we'd be stunned. "Really? BJ?" Now, we'd expect that from any of the other kids, but BJ? That's the kind of kid he grew up as; always wanting to make people happy, make people laugh, make someone's bad day just a little better.

His big brother, Michael, inherited a lot of BJ when he died. Michael does about anything for anyone and expects nothing in return. He'll give you all he has and go hungry. Maybe I made a lot of mistakes raising my children, but when it comes to what matters most, maybe I did a few things right. Or maybe they just had it in them…either way, both are very unselfish, giving individuals who care about everyone.

Facebook Post:
November 16, 2012

"Nudibranchs that feed on hydroids can store the hydroids' nematocysts in the dorsal body wall, the cerata. They can also take in plants' chloroplasts and use them to make food for themselves."

Nick, BJ and Kelli July 2013

A Chosen Son

I bet you were so sad the moment that you knew. That you would soon be leaving earth, I know I felt sad, too. They said that you were comfortable, not in pain or fear. I could hardly find a word to tell my son who would soon be leaving here.

Your dad held up the phone so that you could hear my voice. I hope the words I said that day comforted you and made you rejoice.

Your cancer ridden body was no longer good for you. It wasn't working properly and do what you wanted it to.

I promised you'd find happiness on the other side. I told you not to be afraid, that everyone born has died. I said that you'd be whole again, no longer in pain or sorrow. And soon before you knew it, I'd be with you again tomorrow.

I also said I loved you more than words could ever say. And that if I could I'd trade you places and take the hurt away.

So quickly then you left us, I'm sure you were prepared. I knew there were other members of our family waiting there.

I know once you passed over, you were happy, joyous, and free. The only comfort I can find is in knowing you truly loved me.

And soon my time will come, before I even know it. You'll be waiting on the other side with your arms stretched out to show it.

And in that day we'll understand why God took you so young. It wasn't by mistake, you were a chosen son. You left behind a legacy and didn't even know it. And blessed the lives of many who will forever know it.

Cosmic Dust

The memory of your face, it doesn't go away. I close my eyes and see you each and every day.

I hear your voice the laughter too, the things you used to say. Oh what a shame a boy like you that cancer took away.

You were so smart so talented so full of hopes and dreams. To become a Marine Biologist among many other things.

I sometimes just can't fathom that you are really gone. I find I sleep my life away and sometimes can't go on.

The memories you left behind are with me everywhere. A little boy so sweet so young to grow to see despair.

To have all your dreams shattered, to know you soon would die. Your father by your bedside, it makes me want to cry.

I am so glad I spent with you the last week of your life. To see you as a normal kid, to walk, to eat, and laugh.

But once again the darkness came and you were just exhausted. I had to leave the very next day. I knew you'd soon be gone. I'm grateful not to have seen my baby boy that way. Your siblings did and forever with them it will stay.

So ashes to ashes, dust to dust, you said we are all just cosmic dust. Just tiny drops of water in a never ending sea, but deep within my heart my baby boy you'll always be.

Facebook Post:
September 14, 2011

"The itsy bitsy spider climbed up the water spout. Down came the Goblin and took the spider out."

Almost 9 Months Ago

The morning wakes and you're not there my heart begins to break. Another day without you here, how much more can I take?

I don't want to face what lies ahead; my heart just won't believe it. I close my eyes till I find sleep, once more to relive it.

The things I once found joy in, for I no longer care. Nothing seems to be the same with you no longer there.

My motivation left me the day you said, "Good-Bye." So I only do what's necessary, then either sleep or cry.

It's so hard to make it through the day my joy has all but left me. And when I see your pictures my heart engulfs in misery.

I know you'd want to see me happy but what can I do? Each day that passes by gets harder since the day that I lost you.

Your last few years while on this earth filled with misery and pain. Oh how can a Mother who loved you so much ever find joy again?

My heart just feels so heavy now some days I just want to die. It's just one foot in front of the other and so hard to even try.

It's been almost 9 whole months now since we said our last good byes. I often think about you when I look up at the skies.

I remember sitting at the airport freezing, I knew I'd never see you alive again. I went and bought a Houston hoodie to keep me warm and tried not to think of it then.

But the Lord above forewarned me I knew without a doubt. The day you entered the hospital you were never walking out.

I guess I'm glad he prepared me for what was soon to be. But even with all this knowledge I feel the waves crashing in on me.

This is far too much to bear alone I know I must seek help. I cannot remain in denial so in counseling I have dwelt.

To grieve the loss of a Mother's son, this just isn't supposed to happen. But the Lord knows what He is doing, I just need to learn to trust Him.

I only see a small portion not the whole thing as He can. So until I gain further light and knowledge I'll try and understand.

I know you are in a better place, free from earthly pain. And all the cords that held you bound to your earthly bed.

Now you can walk and even run and probably much more, too. I need to find the inner strength to get through this to be with you.

To live my life happily just the way you'd want it. I know that I will see you again in Gods time, not when I want it.

This time on earth is just a test and goes by very quickly. And in the twinkling of an eye we'll be together eternally.

Just know my son how very proud I was to be your mom. A gift from Heaven God gave to me when I first held you in my arms.

My precious son you were so loved and taught me many things. But most of all that life is short, so love the one's God brings.

Facebook Post:
February 23, 2012

"Just registered for drivers ed"

9 Months Ago

9 months ago you left me. 9 months ago you died. You left me with an empty hollow feeling deep inside.

9 months ago I just returned and you were doing fine. But the nurses did call me saying you were going to die.

At first I did not believe it how could this all be true? Just yesterday I was there visiting with you.

They said that you'd be going home and that you were going fine. For no one saw this coming or I would have stayed a longer time.

But I guess you knew just when to go and what I could not bear. Once I was safely home you left for your home up there.

Knowing I could not bear to see your lifeless body lying there you took your last breath your heart stopped beating and you left for your Heavenly home which God did prepare.

For those of us left have missed you so terribly inside. There isn't a day I don't think of you the love I have for you, the pride.

I said you'd be my baby boy forever and a day. A big boy you did not want to be when your baby sister was on the way.

So through the short years of your life my baby boy you've been. While you were here upon this earth today, tomorrow, and back then.

For that will never ever change, my baby boy you'll always be, I'm so very proud to have been your Mom on earth and for eternity.

Facebook Post:
September 19, 2011

"Off to play Pandemic 2...
Let's hope I can infect Madagascar...."

Get Over It

Written for Janie Budro
Inspired by her son Tyler Lane Budro
who passed away March 10, 2013
shortly before BJ on July 9, 2013

No one understands the pain it doesn't go away. It only gets much harder with each and every day. You want to run back home now, to the way that things once were, and as you trip and stumble your life is just a blur.

How can you just go on knowing all of this is real? How can other's lack compassion for the loss your heart does feel? They think that just because the clock has ticked away another year, that now you should be "over it" they say, "don't shed another tear!"

The hollowness inside of you the emptiness still grows. You try to hide the tears you cry so no one ever knows. But do not be ashamed to feel because your loved one is now gone. It's OK to still be missing him and none of this is wrong.

They just can't understand it if they too have not been there. So when they say "Get over it" it's not their cross to bear.

How hurtful and unkind are those who try to put a limit, on a Mother's grieving heart, who never have been through it. To judge a Mother to show her love she's feeling for her son. A loss so deep most can't comprehend; which never may be done.

We all grieve at our own pace; there's just no reason or rhyme. Some seem to deal quite quickly but for some it just takes more time. So keep in mind that karma is watching over you. It comes back like a boomerang from all you say and do.

And when you judge another, the lack of love not there, may swiftly come upon you to show you her despair. No two will ever grieve the same just as no two children are. Let the healing take its course don't leave mom with a scar.

Talking has its healing powers are you too proud to listen, or do you just prefer when it's you who's reminiscent? Sometimes the best thing you can do is shut up and just listen and let a broken Mother's heart begin to heal. Then maybe you'll have an inkling of how she must really feel.

Then instead of judging her you'll have what's called compassion. You'll learn to love others the way it's meant to happen. It will never be the same she won't be who she was. Forever changed by circumstance for reasons not to judge.

So go about your life and wait till you're in trouble, and when you're faced with similar things just maybe you'll feel sorrow. Sorrow for how you treated her and did not understand. She did not raise two wimpy boys; she raised us up as men.

She was the very best Mother, a boy could ever have, for me to see her unhappy, makes me really sad. It's time for her to move on now and go beyond this pain. But with everyone all judging her, she's still standing in the rain. Let her move on as she please however long it takes; for after all losing a child is rare for Heaven's sake.

Just tell her that I love her and it was just my time to go. And when she makes it to where I'm at, I promise then she'll know. I'm always by her side and even though she cannot see, when she thinks she hears a whisper, it will be coming from me.

***Facebook Post:
March 12, 2012***

"Michael: A dude on a horse! He's gonna pull us over clippidy-clop style!"

Broken

Almost nine months now that you've been gone, the tears have finally come. No longer can I hide my pain or make myself feel numb.

Reality is setting in while I am falling apart. My baby boy forever you'll be, always in my heart.

I miss you more each passing day much more than words can say. The grief inside a mother's heart, that never goes away.

We only learn to live a life without you for awhile. Knowing we will meet again with joy and a new hope for tomorrow.

But even now I know you're near always by my side. You died the very day after I left, for you knew I would have cried.

To see you dead in such a way I never would recover. You waited till I was safely home. I know you loved your mother.

The memories of our last week are bittersweet for sure. Happy moments filled with sorrow knowing you'd soon be leaving here.

Somehow it was a relief to know that you were finally gone. Back to your Heavenly home above with all your suffering done.

The veil is thin I feel you near, each and every day. To be the nerd who always lived in his Mother's basement, you would say.

I guess you finally got your way, I feel you here beside me. Helping to me get my life in order, wanting me to be happy.

I feel your arms around me tight giving me a hug. Whispering in my ears sometimes, "Please don't cry so much."

So as we are together, each and every day. My guardian angel that you are who never went away.

Facebook Post:
September 20, 2011

"I love Netflix instant watch because I love movies... But I love stupid Youtube videos even more :)"

If I Could Die

If others here didn't count on me and I knew I'd be hurting them too. I would have ended my life a long time ago from the pain of losing you.

I just cannot seem to bring back the joy of things in life that once mattered. When I try to comprehend it all I'm overwhelmed and shattered.

How can I go on and live my life, knowing you are gone? How can I smile, laugh and love, when you can't have that at all?

I feel so selfish when I try after all that you went through. I'd sell my soul to the devil if I knew it would bring back you.

My days go by and I don't really care about one thing over another. I'm just living in survival mode, wishing I were someplace or another.

No happiness no sunshine, I live inside a box. I have no friends no family that cares enough to talk.

I long to end this journey here that God had put me through. A lifetime full of misery and now he's taken you.

What's the point in trying or even going on? I do my best for nothing. I'm being punished for being born.

I see no point in continuing a life so full of sorrow. If not today then just perhaps, I'll have the courage tomorrow.

To end my life and all the hell that ever I went through. For very little happiness did I know aside from you.

For now I'll sleep away my life for as long as I can. I'll stay in bed the entire day, for this I know I can.

For only when I'm sleeping do I feel no pain at all. And every once in awhile, in my dreams your name I call.

I wake up crying full of tears but what else can I do? Close my eyes and sleep again, knowing I miss you.

***

I think it was around nine months was when the Novocain began to wear off and things got real. I tried several methods of escape, mostly sleeping as I already had fibromyalgia. I was somewhat suicidal wanting to be with BJ but have read stories from other parents who long to be with their children. We are not crazy, or suicidal. I believe this is just a normal reaction, a thought process of wanting to be with them again so badly, that it gives us a glimmer of hope. We know that if we really needed to badly enough we could be.

However, I know that's not the way it really works and I know how our minds can play tricks on us, especially when depressed and sometimes we may see no other way out. Unfortunately life is pain.

I didn't know the last time I went to Houston and ended up in an InstaCare, diagnosed with laryngitis, that my sickness was related to my son's. I didn't know when I was diagnosed with pharyngitis.

Only this time, the illness had me coughing so much I went to the hospital and wore a mask. I was there maybe ten minutes and had to leave. I was so disappointed. Everything was out of my control but I was there and couldn't even see my own son I was coughing so much. During the days I'd want to sleep till noon and didn't know why, as my mind had other plans but my body refused to pay attention.

It took me fourteen years to finally get a diagnosis...a Neurologist finally gave me the news after I'd been to every kind of doctor there was. He said, "I don't want to offend you but if I can't find anything wrong with you, with the MRI, I'm going to send you to a psychiatrist."

And that's exactly what he did.

He sent me to counseling after putting me on Klonipin, a very highly addictive drug. I was up to 2.5 mg 3 times a day; today I've taken myself mostly off of it. I'm now down to just 1 pill, 3 times a day but when I try to cut back further I have myoclonic seizures.

Basically, I'm in hell either way.

It's a very hard drug to get off of and with my background he never should have put me on it to begin with. The Neurologist diagnosed me as having Somatoform Disorder which is "real, unimagined symptoms brought on by repressed emotional stress." Boy was he off.

Now, fourteen years later, I have a very good doctor here in Utah. He is one of the best who is still trying to find a proper treatment as I am not responding to most. There is no "Gold Standard" treatment available and the goal is to suppress the disease which is progressive, and without treatment, it can be potentially fatal.

Facebook Post:
October 17, 2011

"I wait to fall asleep, then I wait for the bus, wait for class to be over, and then I wait for lunch, where I get to live a little, until the bell then I wait till i go home, wait till theatre practice, wait until its over, then i wait until I fall asleep again.

Ultimately waiting for something that may never happen."

BJ's Celebration of Life

BJ died on July 9th of 2013. He was cremated in Crosby, Texas on the 18th. We waited until we could get everyone who wanted to attend together, and so his celebration of life was held at Bull Sallas Park in New Caney on July the 27th.

We had a pretty good turn-out. People even came after Norm and I had left, bringing with them even more balloons, so there was a second balloon release with messages either inside of, or attached to the balloons for BJ.

We had a batting station and bounce house for the smaller kids, donated by Moonwalks Unlimited and brisket sandwiches you could purchase from the Snack Shack. We also had BJ Car Window decals. There was way more food than anyone could eat.

There were also lots of desserts, especially cupcakes decorated with sea creatures on them. There was a ton of his favorite cheesecake. We could have had a cheesecake party for the entire City of Porter and New Caney, both.

Technically, BJ lived in Porter but attended New Caney High School, the same school named after the astronaut Robert L. Crippen, the same high school my second oldest daughter and BJ's older brother Michael went to and younger sister Kelli is now going to.

New Caney was originally named Presswood after the pioneers who founded it, but 15 to 20 years later it was changed to Caney. The term Caney itself comes from the name of the dense canebrakes that were growing around the nearby Caney Creek, (sugarcane-like thickets). The town was going to be called just Caney, but the first postmaster added the "New" to Caney as there was already a registered city named Caney. And there you have it, from Presswood about 100 years ago, where they raised pigs and cattle and used the H.E.W. Railway; Houston East or West, Hell either way to the locals...to New Caney. New Caney also grew cotton and made syrup. It has always interested me to find out the history behind the names.

For the first time in a very long time I had all of my children together except for BJ; it seemed to surreal. I was still numb, still in shock. I could talk about it easily without crying because to me it wasn't really true. It hadn't really happened. Denial is the first stage of grief and I was in deep. I was not about to let go of my little boy.

He had that adorable, cute little face. He was the teenager who grew his hair long for a short time and had to hold his head back in order to see you. He was the one in the family who outgrew everyone else in height. So he had his sister, his two brothers, two of his three half sisters who were my children and Norm's older daughter we still have not talked to.

The last time we had gotten together this past Thanksgiving, we had everyone together but my second oldest, and Norm's daughter, so five of my six. Because BJ was one of the five, my second oldest took his place at the table. Five of my six babies were all together and possibly for the last time, for all I knew… until we got on the boat.

Facebook Post:
March 11, 2013

"Maybe one day we'll wake up and this will all just be a dream"

(Just before he got sick…in 4 months he'd be gone…)

The Smile

I wake up every morning and put a smile upon my face. A mask to hide my pain and tears from all who see my face.

The pain inside my heart is just too heavy for me to bear. So I go about my day, pretending I don't care.

I act as if I'm over you and that my heart has healed. But it's tattered torn and broken and forever left unreeled.

For no one knows what's underneath and think I'm doing fine. I tell them all that I'm OK but I know that I'm lying.

For each day just gets harder since you went away. But I know you suffered greatly so I'm glad you didn't stay.

I know you're in your home above with your Heavenly Father and Mother. The child I once miscarried, perhaps another brother?

KIMBERLY A. CUTLER

I know now that you are free from pain and the body
that weighed you down, so I go about my busy day
with a smile instead of a frown.

You're happy in your home above but I'm still
missing you. And when I remove the mask each night
I shed a tear or two.

How can another understand such pain and sorrow
too, unless they have traveled a similar road which
took me away from you.

And even though I know that I'll be seeing you again
someday. The pain is so heavy, my stomach in knots,
it just won't go away.

You brought such joy into my life. I never thought
I'd see, the day that I would bury you at Galveston at
sea.

Your body so very strong, in such a short time here so
brief. Then leaving it like a hermit crab, like a shell
upon the beach.

I know you loved the ocean and the Marine life that it
holds. You would have become a Marine Biologist as
your life on earth unfolds.

But instead the Lord decided that your life on earth
was through. You came, you left, you touched many
hearts, you did all you were meant to do.

Only God can understand just why you had to go. As a Mother I love you with all my heart, and I know He loves you more.

For one day we will meet again and tears will be of joy. Then this mask I'll remove for good and really smile with joy.

But until that day there is nothing that anyone can do, to keep my heart from breaking and me from missing you.

Facebook Post:
March 30, 2013 at 8:33 a.m.

"It's called a flame scallop. Actually a clam. And nah Matt I don't like dogs."

Once Upon a Starry Night

Once upon a starry night the waves roll to the shore. They reach the sand where you once played but don't play anymore.

The moon reflects the shadows where you once stood with laughter. Reflecting on what's now emptiness with no more ever after.

The sea shells still are lying there a treasure to be found. But with the waves no laughter now, just silence all around.

What used to be a happy place is now your watery tomb. A life so full of energy has been taken from us too soon.

So we took you to the only place we knew you really loved. We took a boat and left you there, the remains of who we loved.

So on this starry night as the waves roll to the shore, you've temporarily left us, but not forevermore.

We live the lives God gives us then we all are laid to rest. But for you my son, my baby boy, I only want the best.

I know that you'll be happy with the fishes in the sea. For not another place on earth would you rather be.

Your passion was to learn of them to do your very best. To go to school then off to college then a Marine Biologist.

But son God did have other plans and so your life on earth was short. He needed you in Heaven more. For here you were done before you could start.

You left so many broken hearts so sad and in despair. I know that wasn't your intent, with all the love you share.

We know you're in a better place free from pain and sorrow. The only thing that gets me through is to know I'll be seeing you again tomorrow.

Facebook Post: November 18, 2012

"There's only one me, ain't no equivalent"

(A year before his last Thanksgiving when Michael, BJ and Trisha came out to visit).

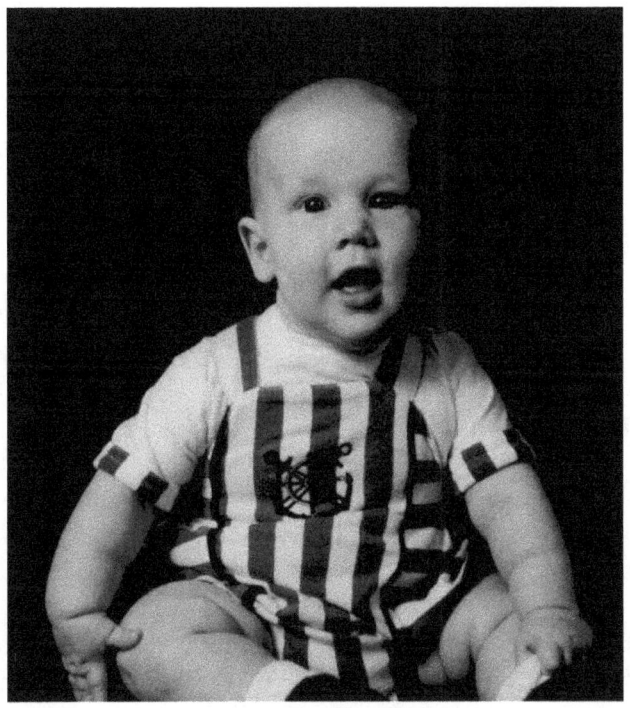

BJ, 5 months, 5 days old

The Boat

So there we were, back in Houston, on a boat leaving Galveston Island to lay BJ to rest. Norm had his remains placed into a bio degradable bag so he would sink to the bottom of the sea. He'd eventually become part of the coral reef. As his dream was to become a marine biologist, I am sure this is what he would have wanted. Yes, BJ loved the ocean, even from that first time at nine-months-old.

We originally wanted to take him to a place called "The Flower Garden" but it was a five hour boat ride both ways. This was only one hour each way. We mostly had some of BJ's friends, JT, Damien, Brittany, his sister, their parents, some of whom I didn't know, two of his favorite teachers and a few more parents, and of course family. This would be the last time our entire family, including me and my six children, would all be together again.

Everyone met on the pier. The captain of the boat chose the spot. She thought BJ might like a place where there was a sunken ship. Ironically, when the boys were much younger, Michael had had two baby showers, one in which he received a green and white sailor looking outfit with a captain's wheel and an anchor on the front.

We had Michael's picture taken in this outfit when he was five days and five-months-old and thought it would be fun to do the same; to have BJ's picture taken in the exact same outfit at five months and five days old. They both looked so adorable yet uniquely different. I have those 8x10's in a large picture frame that once hung on the wall when they were much younger. And I still have the outfit.

At one point in time, Norm bought me a special ceramic picture frame with a raccoon, bunny, dog, bear and pig on the bottom front of it. So this, along with one other ceramic pictures of Kelli were the only two pictures in special frames that didn't eventually get packed away as the kids grew older.

It was a sunny day. The weather was pleasant, and as we boarded the Texsun II I remember one of Norm's friends holding the small tan box, which was all that was left of what used to be my son. My mind could not comprehend such a thing. I didn't want to even touch it. It was gross and disgusting; it wasn't my son!

The boat was of medium size, it could hold between 100 to 150 people. It had a deck to walk around and a cabin underneath if you wanted to get out of the storm, I suppose, in bad weather. It also served as a restaurant for longer trips. There were also comfortable benches and a restroom.

Some of those attending had chosen to stay out on the deck while other's waited in the cabin below. There I sat. Norm's friend had sat the box down for awhile, which he had been previously guarding with his life. I sat at the dining table and stared at it, what used to be my son…in a box. I read the words on the cover. Those words, how they sunk into my very soul. It all seemed so surreal. Not possibly my son.

Finally, I touched it. It wasn't as yucky as I had imagined, yet still it wasn't my son. I had to get away. I went to the back of the boat.

It seemed like it took hours to reach our destination. The somber mood was everywhere. I sat on the back deck with my feet up on a railing, and just watched the other boats go by. Most were much larger than ours. The wind seemed to blow through me although it wasn't cold. I just kept waiting; looking down at the water, trying to take everything in…this wasn't really happening.

That was it! Soon I'd wake up in my bed and get a call saying BJ was off the oxygen, back to his physical therapy, getting stronger.

Suddenly startled by the sound of the motor shutting off, I awoke as if from a bad dream. But it was real. The scary monsters were there, all the bad things in the dream you dreaded were now all about to come true. The boat came to a sudden stop as did my heart. Everyone gathered towards the back where I had sat alone. One of my daughters took a video of the ceremony.

My ex and I had both unintentionally chosen to wear orange shirts that day. BJ's favorite color, unless it had changed. It was disheartening to see everyone's faces look so sad, and mine so very lost. Norm said a few words, then gently took what was left of his beloved son and gently lowered the bag into the ocean as he told him, "I love you, buddy."

He wiped tears from his face and we all stood a moment longer, then everyone seemed to go away, some to the front of the boat, the teachers to the side deck, I think to give the family some privacy. The rest went down into the cabin. I just sat there in disbelief.

I'm not sure it really sank in for anyone that day. When BJ was in ICU, most of his friends hadn't gotten a chance to see him. And as what would have been BJ's senior year, started, there were several kids who didn't even know where BJ was or what had happened. This was before I was diagnosed with the Mucus Membrane Pemphagoid, during the time BJ was in the hospital.

We started off again, heading back to shore. For a brief moment of insanity I wanted to leap into the water and save my son. I was frantic! I couldn't understand why everyone was suddenly going their own way leaving BJ behind as if he didn't matter. As if they could just discard him as a piece of trash to be thrown away and forgotten about....I NEEDED to get to him!!!

Luckily my daughter was there. "But Mom, he's not there," she said.

She was right and I knew it. That wasn't my son. That was what remained of his body. His spirit lived on in a happier place. He was free like a bird now. Had God even taken him anywhere yet or was he right there beside me, with us all, the entire time watching? If we could see what we cannot see, then maybe we could finally see.

"God, remember the gift?" I thought to myself. "How can you give me a gift to be able to have more children just to take them away? It's not fair. I want him back. I need him more than you do."

And in that very moment I needed to grasp onto something, anything, to capture that moment in time, something I felt would give me a piece of him. I needed something tangible that I could touch, feel, and hold on to.

Then I saw it.

I wasn't quite sure what "it" was but I grabbed it and held on. The thing weighed maybe 2 pounds or less. I told my daughter, "I'm stealing this, I have to." I put it in my pocket. It was small enough and I knew nobody would miss it. After all, this boat was lined with these things, whatever they were. But this one was mine, a piece of that moment in time I could hold onto and remember my baby boy forever as I had nothing else left.

Once docked, I went to the gift shop called Murdock's and purchased a Galveston Island T-Shirt. I didn't want to ever ruin it so I have only worn it once, on BJ's 18th birthday. I also bought a mood necklace which turns green, blue, purple, and has the same symbol on the front as his baby outfit. The necklace includes an anchor with a captain's wheel.

As soon as I got back to my hotel room I had to call my husband back in Salt Lake City and tell him that I stolen something. I couldn't handle the guilt and had to make it right. He asked me what it was.

I said, "I don't know."

"You don't know?" he replied. I tried to explain it to him and he figured it out. We were on what was known as a deep sea ocean liner used for deep sea fishing. This was a weight to help the line sink to the bottom of the ocean floor. Now I get the term, "Hook, line and sinker."

He said not to worry, that we'd call once I got home and pay for it or find a way to replace it or send it back. When I finally got a hold of the captain and told her who I was and what I'd done she was so sweet. She told me not to even worry about it. She just wanted the number off of it so she could put another in its place. I still have the weight and forever will. Some things people treasure.....it sits just above me here on my desk from where I write.

Know that I am not a writer. I am a mom. I am not a poet. I am a mom. I have barely worked in my life because I decided to be a "Stay Home Mom" and that is about all I really know how to do. I've struggled in writing this and deleted large portions several times and had to re-do them, and found duplicates and had to re-copy things I'd accidently delete etc. etc. etc. BUT...I fulfilled my goal and my gift to BJ of fulfilling his wish as to not be forgotten.

I quit smoking and started walking which turned into jogging, which turned into the gym with its several machines. Maybe that's what inspired BJ to work out as he did.

After BJ went into the hospital I lost 35 pounds. I have not been to the gym once and cannot get myself motivated. When he died a part of me went with him. For those of you who have never lost a child, a sibling, or loved one…grief is a difficult thing.

We all react differently. No two people grieve the same just as no two children are the same. Some get through it rather quickly, for others it seems to take more time but I feel for most it never goes away. Without that person in your life you just learn to live differently.

I like to compare separation to a family sending a son or daughter off to war. Let's say you don't get to talk to them at all. After three months you really miss them. After six months you miss them even more. Do you think just because a year goes by you'd miss them any less? Of course not, the longer they are gone, the more you yearn to have them back, the more you miss them. The harder life becomes living without them.

My daughter found the entry on BJ's Facebook page about how he wanted to be remembered, how he didn't know how much time he had left but he'd stick around a while longer, but in return we weren't to forget him…especially all his Facebook friends. That is what inspired me to write this book.

You know, it's a funny thing, but I truly believe that BJ is not far away. I read a book about death, and because of this book as well as many people who have shared their experiences with me during a grief counseling course I took, I know our loved ones are not far away. They often come to us in different ways to let us know they are okay.

I had an experience after the boat took off and everyone left. There were a gazillion seagulls that swarmed the boat. They just kept coming to the back and would go back a-ways then come back again over and over. I was so amazed and mad at myself that I didn't know how to work the video portion on my phone. It was so incredible, I had never seen anything like it - ever. The seagulls followed one another for such a great distance.

It's the simple things that can remind you.

I was once at a meeting and there was a young kid there wearing a black shirt and a bright red pair of tennis shoes. How many people do you know who own bright red tennis shoes? I was later to learn this kid with the dirty blonde hair was named Ben (Benjamin, my BJ) …I was stunned.

In July of 2014 I went to a *Journey* concert. We were sitting on the grass listening as other bands were playing before they came on. I was missing BJ and feeling sad. All of a sudden in front of me someone was passing through. All I saw was a bright red pair of tennis shoes, right before me almost in my lap. I quickly glanced up but whoever it was had gone, but in the distance I saw two lone seagulls fly by at just that very moment.

It made me smile.

Facebook Post:
November 8, 2011

"You're Amazing Just Shut Up And Remember That"

A Mother's Grief

Sometimes the world around me seems dark and full of gloom. Your memory still haunts me of how you died too soon.

I thought I'd see you so much more, when I moved away. But time went on without me seeing you anyway.

You'll never understand the guilt which lies within my heart. I left you as a child never meaning for us to part.

You truly are the greatest gift that God has given me. To be your Mother while on this earth, and for all eternity.

The times we shared are priceless and I never will forget. I wish I could have traded places with you all the while that you were sick.

Seeing you so strong, so healthy and handsome as could be. The thought of you dying from cancer just never occurred to me.

You were so smart and talented among the very best. They tell me up in Heaven there's a new Marine Biologist.

Your body got so tired, in such a very short time. It withered away to nothing as your organs slowly died.

We had your body cremated for burial at sea. I hope your found this pleasant, and a place you'd like to be.

The moment the boat left you there I was no longer me. I will never be the same without you, no matter how hard I try to be.

Not having you in my life now, every day I cry. And times I just cannot go on and wish that I too could die.

"Cheer up and be happy" I can hear you say, but how could a loving Mother leave her son that way?

For now I'll go on pretending with a smile upon my face. Though my heart bleeds for you with anguish, nothing can ever erase.

I missed the last years of your life but so glad I was there, that very last week you were here on earth yet still I'm in despair.

A Mother's anguish I have found will never go away.
So until I see you again my son, silently I'll pray. I'll
pray to Heavenly Father, to help you understand that
day.

I didn't mean to desert you, I thought I had a plan.

Please know how much I love you, for you must - you
are so cleaver. Until we meet again you'll be my baby
boy forever.

Facebook Post:
November 3, 2011

"We are all just a hair, meaningless alone, but we all
must function together to make the great hair-do of
life. Philosophized"

Don't Cry a Tear For Me

Sometimes when I'm alone at night I feel your presence near. I feel you tell me it will be OK to hold on and be strong today.

I feel your arms around me saying, "Mom please don't cry." "I know I left this mortal world but my spirit didn't die."

"I'm still right here beside you though you cannot see my face, I'm happy now and free from pain and in a lovely place."

"Please don't cry because of me for I'm not really gone. If you could see beyond the veil, each day you would be strong."

"For not another tear you'd shed, there'd be no reason why." "Your days would just be filled with joy and no more would you cry."

"For God has a reason for everything He does, He loves us unconditionally. Why? Just because. You'd know that things are just the way that they are meant to be.

"If you could see beyond the veil and see the real me." But I know that that's impossible, right now you cannot see. So just a whisper in your ear, don't cry a tear for me."

Facebook Post: November 11, 2011

"This weekend sure seems promising. Let's have a blast.

Of course I'm right, I'm Ben! I used to think that the show was stupid, but after actually WATCHING it I fell in love with it.

It makes me feel smart when I figure out stuff before they do:)"

Forgotten

December the 15th. You came into this world. Most of your birthdays all but forgotten with Christmas lurking near.

Too busy buying gifts for others, no one noticed "you." One gift to buy for your birthday was all they had to do.

So many parties empty when no one even came. Too much going on elsewhere and Christmas was to blame.

Just 17, to celebrate while you were on this earth. If I could I'd go back in time and change the date of your birth.

I'd change it to another day where nothing was going on. And all who were invited would surely come along. We'd make it the biggest party, a day to celebrate "YOU", for you'd be the most important one and there'd be nothing better to do.

So now gone but not forgotten a request you made long ago. On your Facebook page, perhaps you knew you soon would go.

2 years before you even got sick you asked us not to forget you. You're gone but not forgotten and remembered in all we do.

Although I'm not a writer, in honor of your request, I've chosen to write this book and to do my very best.

It's not for money or for fame nor riches of any kind. It's just a way to show that you were here, if even for a very short time. A way for all to remember for the many hearts you touched. Some of whom you knew so well, some not so much.

Some who never even met you shed a tear or two. For that 17 year old boy with cancer, whose lives were touched by you.

You had a way of being there for all who knew you well. You wanted everyone to be happy, you truly cared and they could tell.

So even though your birthday's come and gone by the last time here. We'll celebrate your Heavenly Birthday and remember you every year.

For in Heaven you will never be forgotten you are loved far too much. In time we'll be together again, and honor each day with love.

Facebook Post:
November 13, 2011

"How many of you would drink this liquid? "Like" if you would NOT.
is called "hydroxyl acid", the substance is the major component of acid rain.
contributes to the "greenhouse effect".
may cause severe burns.
is fatal if inhaled.
contributes to the erosion of our natural landscape.
accelerates corrosion and rusting of many metals.
may cause electrical failures and decreased effectiveness of automobile brakes.
has been found in excised tumors of terminal cancer patients.
everyone who comes in contact with it is known to die"

The Tradition

Just as we'd celebrated BJ's 18th Birthday worldwide with many friends online through Facebook etc. we decided to celebrate again for his 19th Birthday.

We decided to start a new tradition. On Thanksgiving 2012, BJ's last Thanksgiving on this earth, we'd celebrated with his older brother, Michael, and Trish, his girlfriend.

But BJ, well, he was still around in spirit and so we invited him to be with us again. We sat out an empty plate at the head of the table next to his brother, Nick. As we hadn't done this the previous year, Nick thought it was quite odd. I think he may have thought we were nuts but hey, everyone does this right? Ha-ha.

So, about half way through the meal, (entirely cooked by my husband Steve as I am rarely allowed in "his" kitchen, even to clean) Nick announced that he was going up to his room to get some sanity. I found it quite humorous yet a bit sad. He just didn't grasp what we were trying to do.

After the meal, we took a couple of throwaway plates and packed them full of ham, turkey, stuffing, mashed potatoes and gravy, green bean casserole, and candied yams. In a separate bag we placed lots of homemade wheat rolls. Then, on another plate we placed a large piece of pumpkin pie with whipped cream.

I said a prayer before we left asking for guidance and we were on our way.

We drove from our home in Kearns to downtown Salt Lake City. We searched for a homeless man and finally found him. There he was. He was a black man about 40 something. He walked with a slight limp. He was carrying his backpack along with a rolled up sleeping bag which was obviously his bed. He'd stopped on the corner waiting for the light.

I called him over. "Have you eaten yet?" I asked him.

"I have not," he replied. He was missing a few teeth.

I proceeded to hand him all of the food, along with an extra coat we had to help keep him warm even though he had one on. It gets so cold in Utah. I explained to him why we were giving him the food and who it was from.

After my explanation I could tell he was deeply touched and it gave me warm fuzzies all over. The feeling was like Christmas and it gave me an idea.

We now plan on doing this on Christmas as well every year so that BJ's memory can continue to live on. It's rewarding to serve others who benefit with what he can no longer share here on this earth;

knowing, at the same time, that he will have a much more bountiful feast in Heaven.

I don't normally share good deeds done and feel you receive more blessings if done in secret but this was different; this was a new tradition to honor and remember BJ for the loving caring and giving soul he was.

Now, even in death, the memory of his life will go on blessing others in need for years and years to come.

Facebook Post:
November 14, 2011

"Facebook: What's on your mind?
Me: I don't know what to think about anything any more."

Empty Heart

The days keep moving forward, even though you're gone. I try to picture you above, free from pain yet full of love.

Your last days here were not the best, by the memories I'm still haunted.
To see the boy I loved so much, suffer so undaunted.

You never complained through all your sufferings and I'm sure your fear. The bravest soul I've ever known, in my heart I'll always hold you dear.

I miss you in so many ways no one can understand except another parent who has lost a child can.

The emptiness inside my heart will never go away. I miss you more with all my heart, each and every day.

I know one day we'll meet again, never to depart.
Until that day the emptiness remains within my heart.

Letting Go

If letting go means holding on that's all that I can do.
To cherish every moment on this earth I had with you.

But I have to let you go now and leave you in God's care. And give thanks to Him with all my heart for the time I had you here.

Your life on earth has ended God has another plan.
Your work is far from over it's just in another land.

The days ahead I'll miss you but I know I'll soon be there. With you in that other land for us that our God did prepare.

For this life here on earth is short, a test for us to bear; to see if we are faithful and just where we'll go from here.

There really is no sadness if you truly understand, for life goes on beyond the veil just in another land.

I know my time too will come much sooner than I think. And when it does you'll be there waiting at the gate.

The joy we'll feel will overcome the sadness I once felt. And wash away all the tears I cried for you and comfort all my guilt.

So now I'll turn you over to a loving God who cares. He brought you here then took you home through a veil of tears.

Your life now ever after is happy evermore. The son I loved so dearly, pain never again to endure.

You fought to the very end and not once did you complain. You'll always be my hero. You took a lot of pain.

You were so brave to the very end and I think you knew it, too. That our loving Father in Heaven had a Mansion prepared for you!

Facebook Post:
November 28, 2011

"After the most amazing Thanksgiving break imaginable, I am back home."

NOT...The End!

I thought I was finished writing this book.

    I am sitting here in my Salt Lake City home basement bedroom typing...while the cover is finally coming to life after all these months. Tom Siller had agreed to do the work long ago. It was I who procrastinated.

    I postponed writing this book several times, when the pain become too much to bear and I couldn't wrap my brain around the reality of it any longer. There were times I had to turn all of his pictures upside down so I could no longer look at the stark reminder of him.

    Those on the wall I had to cover up.

    The shirt with the red, black and yellow flames coming from the bottom up, I found so disturbing. Every time I'd open my bottom dresser drawer, I'd remember that it was given to his older brother Michael a long time ago by a neighbor. It was a silky black bottom up shirt. The same one he had gotten his 5th Grade picture taken in.

    It sat there in the drawer as if to taunt me. "I am the devil now devouring your child, as he has been cremated," it said to me. Later I handed the shirt down to his younger brother, Nicholas, who eventually ripped it so I washed it and gently put it away.

I told my husband about a dream I'd had, and swore that it wasn't a dream, that it was more real than a dream. BJ was in frustration because he was not able to communicate. He was upset but not at me. He continued trying to talk to me, yet he couldn't. It was like visiting him again at the hospital after hearing I had a very, very, very sick little boy; the time I'd flown out to Houston the very next day and discovered my boy on life support, barely speaking.

The things he was saying I couldn't make out anyway.

His hand wasn't working and he couldn't text me. He was getting so very frustrated, unable to communicate. Then suddenly, in the dream, I made out the words. It's as if he was saying, "Finish my book, finish my book!"

Later I thought he might have been saying, "Finish my work, finish my work!" so I rushed to complete them both. I finished the book and my husband Steven, in proxy for BJ, took out his Temple Endowments. I had the distinct impression that in not doing these things for him, he was stuck. He needed me to do them so he could move on...

So, this morning, December 10, 2014, I saw him again in a dream, only he wasn't lying in a bed unable to communicate. As I slowly came out of this dreamlike state upon awakening, we were talking, laughing, and he was so happy. He was whole and able to communicate clearly and his expression of joy just made me cry, but they were happy tears. He was so grateful for what I had done.

I started talking to him out loud instead of in my mind as I continued waking up. I told him I'd sell the heck out of this book and continue to do things that would ensure he would always be remembered and never forgotten. He was just so thrilled.

I awoke fully, rubbed my teary eyes and BJ slowly faded away, but I was happy.

The dream made me realize the injustice of the title on the cover. BJ's story was a short lived one. He died and now he's gone. But he's still as real and with us today as he was ever before. There are so many things the eye cannot see. There are so many of God's ways that our minds are not ready to fully understand.

The day my husband Steve went to the temple I'd been tanning. I remember feeling horrible as I was coming off high doses of prednisone, probably too quickly, which was causing me to have miserable withdrawal. Oh, how I hate drugs!

I was driving home, down the very street he'd once traveled with me, sitting beside me, his brother Michael and Trisha in the back. And just like two years ago I *felt* him there. In my mind I knew it wasn't so but I glanced over just to be sure and saw nothing. Still, his presence was so strong it was beyond denial.

I thought I must be going crazy. After all, the steroids had been making me a super bi-polar, psycho manic and very aggressive towards even strangers. I often feared just what would come out of my mouth but I still felt him with me so very strongly.

I kept glancing over to the empty seat, then happened to briefly look up at the sky. All of a sudden there were two sea gulls, flying in an up and down pattern almost as if they were dancing. Ha! Seagulls! Those birds I kept seeing out of nowhere and in random locations at times when I was missing him or thinking about him.

It was then it hit me with such force. "Mom, I accepted the gift, thank you," I heard BJ say.

What Steve had done for him in the temple was a very spiritual gift that BJ could not have done alone now that he was dead, yet he still had the option of accepting or denying that which was given to him as a gift on this day, December 13, 2014.

He wanted me to know he had accepted and was very happy.

I broke down and bawled all the way home. I couldn't get myself together, wondering if passengers in other cars might be noticing me, though I didn't really care.

I continued looking for seagulls the rest of the way home, but saw none. I did, however, see many flocks of black birds.

This book is not truly BJ's story. Just a very small portion of his life here on this earth because BJ continues to live on, in another realm, like leveling up on a video game on the other side of the veil where mortal man cannot see.

Oh, but BJ is still so very real and more alive than ever. And, I guarantee you, he is happier and wiser than any of the people he has met while on this earth. He came to this earth and learned what he needed to learn, while the rest of us are still trying to figure stuff out. He did what he promised his Father in Heaven he would do and so now he has moved on to a much greater work.

He will forever remain a part of us until we all see him again someday, when our time comes. Until then, he doesn't want us to be sad. As he quoted on his Face Book wall,

BJ Crawford
November 7, 2011
*"Don't worry too much about life-
Nobody comes out alive."*

BJ was a smart, handsome young man who cared about people and lived a good life. He was funny and can be remembered for so much more than what he's asked to be remembered for. He taught me so much about life, so much more than I ever taught him as a mother.

KIMBERLY A. CUTLER

Acceptance

My son if I could tell you all the nights I've cried.
The times I've laid in bed at night and asked myself just why.

The memories of you haunt me to see you so frail and thin. When just before you left us, you were a strong and buff young man.

I try not to think of what you did endure and the visits to the hospital remind me even more.

It seems like only yesterday but nearly 9 months now. And how I've managed this far I'll never quite know how.

I know I'll need some help to get me through the phases. For grief if often long and hard and sometimes never ceases.

Denial is so very strong when you don't want it to be real. But 9 months is a long time now and it's time for me to feel.

I know the anger's coming, I feel it oftentimes. I can't control when it will show, it just bursts out of rhyme.

Then bargaining I hear is next I'll promise God anything. Just to have one more day with you and make this all a dream.

But once I truly realize that never will be so, depression then will set it and then I'll really know.

Acceptance is still the answer to all my problems today. So I guess I can apply that to the day God took you away.

No man without legs can grow new ones any more than I can bring you back. So until we meet again my son, acceptance is where it's at.

Facebook Post:
December 31, 2011

"Traintracks at night. I love fweedom."

Adventures with Scott
by Scott Tatum, a friend

I met BJ at the James Coney Island in Humble Texas, the location of the original Humble Pokémon league, where I had been a regular for some time. It was late in the year, I think it was around December 2010, and the newest Pokémon games, HeartGold and SoulSilver had been out for several months.

    I had a good team of Pokémon, and nobody at the league could beat me. The league owner told me that I needed to play the new guy, a kid a few years younger than me with a long, dark mop-head hair, and a blue Nintendo DSI. We played a couple of matches; I won the first, but lost badly the second time around. Given that I had the reputation back then as being the most obsessed with competitive play, anyone being able to beat me was a feat, and BJ earned my instant respect; we swapped friend codes and planned to play online later.

    In the following months we bonded over mutual love for playing the deceptively deep Pokémon game series. BJ also got into the trading card game, and we frequently swapped ideas for better decks at the two weekly Pokémon leagues.

BJ soon became better than me at the card game, and we both remained equals at the video games, although we both became much better, eventually learning a little known trick to control the random factor of the games, legally giving us Pokémon for our teams that would literally take mere mortals thousands of hours to procure. In the Houston Pokémon community at this time we may have been the first two people to be able to do this consistently.

In the summer of 2011, we took a road trip together to the United States Pokémon National Championships. It was me, my brother Matthew, BJ, and James Mckinney ('JT') and my mom, captain of the GMC Yukon xl.

The trip took us all the way from the Houston area to Indianapolis, and I think it would be accurate to say that there was hardly ever a dull moment through the whole thing. The night before the start of the event we celebrated a Japanese holiday: "Tanabata", which involved writing wishes on a piece of paper, and burning them at midnight. I don't remember my wish, in all honesty, but BJ's wish was very memorable: "I wish for a REAL adventure!"

At midnight we lit them up; the sharpie ink caught and the paper was ashes in seconds. The tournament had over one thousand people, and was a three-day blast; we didn't finish that high, but we did ok. We all played in several of the side-events, and won some of them, especially the mini video game tournaments.

After the event was over we went to the hotel pool and relaxed for a few hours. On the way home we stopped for the night at my grandparents, because they were conveniently located, and we were over our hotel budget. We had a few hours before dark to wander around and give BJ and JT the grand tour of the fairly large property.

Around sunset, near a small pond, Matthew ordered JT to stand still, telling him there was a snake right by him. In a fairly adrenaline packed moment, we killed the poisonous Copperhead with a hunting knife I was carrying. By the time we made it back to the cabin we were spending the night in, we were in agreement that we had satisfied the requirements of having had a real adventure.

That night we talked about all kinds things; we had the deepest and most open minded discussion about our families and our religious beliefs that I've ever been part of, despite us having very different religious backgrounds. The ride home the next day was sleepy and uneventful, other than us planning to make a zombie apocalypse video game.

Eventually BJ drifted out of the competitive sphere of Pokémon, but we stayed in touch and played "Minecraft" (another fun, deceptively complex game) on a server he'd built, and met in real life to hang out or see a movie on occasion, and experience the occasional Pokémon video game battle.

I followed the cancer battle on Facebook, not being able to visit in person, (not being family, the hospital wouldn't allow it). I was able to talk to BJ a little bit on the messenger at least.

I remember the July morning when my knees hit the floor... That's all I have to say about that...

I doubt I'll ever have a friend like BJ again; he was an unlikely bundle of contradictions personality wise, somehow arrogant and politely respectful all at the same time. I'll never forget BJ or the adventures we had back then. I remember him every time I dust off my old Pokémon games, or drive by the Denny's on I-59, where the old Kingwood Pokémon league was held. He will be missed, and he will be remembered.

Rest in peace, forever in our hearts, Benjamin Crawford.

Your friend, Scott Tatum.

Facebook Post
December 31, 2011

"Last fun was so night!"

Beforehand

Just like the elusive butterfly somehow all sleep eludes me. And when I try to sleep again the thought of you intrudes me.

How can I rest? How can I sleep when you are all alone? Knowing all you've been through to reach your Heavenly Home.

Such a sweet young handsome man, why did you have to die? I ask myself most every day and always wonder why.

A perfect life ahead of you so full of hopes and dreams. Taken all too suddenly and unexpectedly.

Just yesterday it seems you were here and all the fun we had. The places we all went seemed like a dream but now leave me feeling sad.

Your memory still lingers on with every breath I take. Oh child of mine you were so brave to die for cancer's sake.

I guess the Lord prepared me, I remember the day I knew. It was long before the others, I almost told them too.

I kept it down within my soul, just hoping things would change. But just as sure as life moved on, I knew I could not rearrange.

For God had told me beforehand so that I would be prepared. And the last day that I saw you alive I knew I couldn't be scared.

For what he told me came to pass as no one else could see. And all along no one knew the answers he had given to me.

The last thing that you said to be before I walked away, was "Good-Bye Mom, I love you." Then you died the very next day.

I knew then when you said those words I would not see you again. A pang went through my soul that night which confirmed all I had been given.

It took awhile yet to admit that you had truly died. And as the days went on and on it got even more painful inside.

I thank the Lord for loving me enough to let me know. For preparing me for your death before I let you go.

Although the pain is still the same it's easier to bear. I know now for a certainty in Heaven you'll be there. I'm thankful for the gospel and the truths that lie within. He only took you for a moment, soon we'll be together again!

Facebook Post:
January 22, 2012

"Atleast I can always rely on myself"

Finding Balance

My heart just can't embrace the thought that you're no longer here. I look into the past and I see you everywhere.

I hold you in my heart and I will never let you go. Too afraid of moving forward, fear I'll leave you all alone.

But I know I must move forward with a life forever changed. A new perspective of what will be, different not the same.

Torn apart by life from death cancer took you away too soon. If I could just have you for one more day I'd promise you the moon.

I don't know how to let go though and leave the past behind. Just how do you move forward when your 17 yr old son has died?

For children are not supposed to die my mind cannot comprehend. The grief I can bear just a little at a time until I'm on the mend.

It comforts me a bit to know I'll see you again someday. The Lord God gave you to me then He took your life away.

You're in a better place now, no sorrow pain or fear. The precious moments together I will always hold them dear.

Who would have ever thought that it was possible to say, my son just 17 years old died of cancer today?

It came on all too sudden and it took you very fast. I know I must move forward holding dearly to the past.

I need to find a balance to look forward and behind. God only takes the very best and you were one of a kind. So forward I shall go while holding dearly to the past. To find that perfect balance until we're together at last.

I cannot get stuck within my grief with joy no longer there I just need to learn how to live differently and face the burdens I'll bear.

More on the Secret Life of Plants, Pocket Stones, and the Pineal Gland

The Secret Life of Plants:
Have you ever heard of people who talk to their plants and the plants seem to thrive? Perhaps that's with good reason. The subject itself is quite complicated, but to keep it simple: A picture would be taken of a leaf, which would have an aura around it or a glow.

After taking the photo, those researching the phenomena would tear the leaf in half and immediately take another photo (Kirlian photography); the aura would *still* be showing in the photograph. This energy field or aura meant it had life, therefore, even though it did not have a heart or brain (some scientists believe) plants have emotions.

The Secret Life of Plants is a controversial video/book/documentary about experiments revealing unusual phenomena.

Crystals and Pocket Stones:

All quartz crystals have six primary properties. They are able to store, structure, amplify, focus, transform, and transmit energy, which includes matter, emotion, thought, and information.

One of the most effective, easiest and tangible alternative therapies available is called chakra healing. You can do this yourself at home at a fraction of the cost of other therapies.

Crystal healing means this natural frequency helps to restructure, harmonize, our electro-magnetic and physical bodies, restoring order to dysfunctional metabolisms. Quartz crystal has a precisely defined natural frequency at which it oscillates.

Crystal healing has been recorded by older cultures in some form or another, mostly with deep rooted belief systems which supported holistic ideas and methods. Crystal healing has largely become an area of 'Faith and Flakiness' without this cultural foundation.

Quartz crystals have been used in ritual healings throughout history; one of the seven precious substance's of Buddhism. In the oldest writings on earth, the Sanskrit literatures of ancient India, quartz crystals are named Bhisma-Ratna, the gem that removes fear.

The Celtic Quartz of Wales and Ireland is an exceptionally energetic healing crystal.

Many books have been written on the subject of crystals, their properties and underlying principles. Why crystals really are *Stones of Power* are often completely neglected. Although it may be a mystery, it's no secret.

Vedic astrology, or Jyotish in Sanskrit, translates as the Science of Light, an ancient astrological discipline that originated more than 5000 years ago in ancient India. The Sanskrit, meaning "seers" understood the correlation between themselves, the universe, and the Divine.

Perhaps the most misunderstood, least used, and most often ignored area relating to crystal healing and the metaphysical uses of gemstones is the correlation between astrology and gemstones.

The chakras are subtle dynamic energy vortexes and are just as much a part of our bodies as our arms and legs. Just like electricity, you cannot see it but when you turn on the light, you can see its effect. The chakras can similarly be understood by their effects.

I have recently turned to pocket stone crystals, having recently received them in the mail. I have decided to learn more about how to use them for healing purposes. The package is a beautiful assortment of nine different stones.

The aquamarine stone is my favorite as it stands for sea water. When I read of its healing powers, I discovered it was called the *throat stone*; it's exactly what I need.

Who says the Chinese don't know something we have set aside as we pour toxic pharmaceutical drugs into our bodies? These drugs cause more problems than we can get rid of, and there's a list of side-effects and ingredients, things we don't even know what they are.

Drugs are a band-aid not a cure. Natural cures are what BJ and I both needed, though I, at first, saw the natural way of healing a bit differently. But trying BJ's methods excites me.

Flair-ups from my Mucus Membrane Pemphagoid (a blistering auto immune disease) still occur for me off and on as my disease continues to progress. This last round of high dose prednisone turned me into the psycho B----- from h---! I yelled at people, cussed them out, and wished them death. So not like me.

That's when I turned to stone crystals.

Because of my health issues, I have also had experience with the Bio Energy Synchronization Technique. B.E.S.T. Chiropractic offers eastern medicine; they are not like a traditional chiropractor at all. B.E.S.T. is also unlike Reiki but somewhat similar. Acupuncture is also used.

After just a visit or two my 80-year-old feeling body feels 20 again, despite my fibromyalgia, which hasn't bothered me again for a very long time after I've had the work done. It's only when I have a flair up from my auto immune disease that my fibromyalgia is set off.

My doctor is truly amazing and trained from a Chinese expert. His secretary was in a horrible car accident and he helped her with just a few visits. She has now been working for him over 20 years. Now, after seeing how amazing this eastern medicine was, her son then studied for it and now works there also.

He has been there for over 10 yrs. He can just wave his hand over certain parts of my body and tell me traumatic experiences that happened at a certain age and hit the nail on the head every time; things he would have no way of knowing from just the top of his head. He has also told me where my emotional scars are and so much more.

My doctor has spoken about the third eye. He has also spoken about the chia seed; it's not just a plant inside a ceramic animal growing fur, it's a super food, long ago nick-named the runner's food. The seed has many powerful nutrients.

God has put so much on this earth for use to heal our bodies. God did not put all the prescription drugs together that we pay a fortune for at the pharmacy. Man made those, and men fail us.

The Pineal Gland: Your Third Eye

What's in your toothpaste? Are you ready for your child to get that fluoride treatment? And why are they adding it to the water?

Now some doctors are saying fluoride causes cancer, and that fluoride causes it faster than any other chemical. Fluoride is so toxic it is considered Hazardous Waste by the EPA. Crest became the first fluoride toothpaste in 1955. Ever read the label? If swallowed call the poison control center! Honestly now, you mean to tell me kids are not going to be swallowing this garbage?

Hitler put fluoride in the water in the concentration camps. I doubt he wanted them to have healthy cavity-free teeth. It was used to sedate them. Why, oh why, are we using it in our drinking water, our toothpaste and giving our children fluoride treatments? It's the same ingredient found in rat poison and Prozac. Fluoride calcifies your pineal gland. This third eye literally has rods and cones just like your other eyes.

The pineal gland is located inside a 'cave' behind the pituitary gland. It produces melatonin, a hormone that regulates daily body rhythms. It is known as the master gland which governs our third eye and the center of psychic awareness in the human mind.

It physically affects every system in your body and has the potential to determine the expansion or contraction of your psychic awareness, consciousness, and experience with the divine. This is something that has been around for many years. Inside pyramids there are drawings of the pineal gland and cultures who even today mark their forehead with a dot to symbolize this third eye.

On this topic, I could go on and on, but my knowledge is very limited compared to the vast amount of information BJ and his brother Michael gained in such a short time. They are both exceptionally smart along with their youngest brother Nicholas! And of course their sister Kelli is equally as smart.

I am very proud of all of my children, especially my oldest son, Michael. Life has not been easy for him. He's been through a lot; has endured many things most kids will never in their lifetime have to experience, and now he has the loss of his brother who has both broken him and made him a stronger person - broken him because his best friend and lifelong buddy is no longer with him, strengthened him because the reality is, he never left his side.

BJ had knowledge beyond his years. He had a view of the universe and how all things work together, body, mind, and spirit. Along with BJ's big brother, Michael, BJ has opened my eyes to an even greater understanding of the universe. I know the day will come for all of us as all born must one day die, and only a few come into this world already knowing some of the things others have to wait for and learn later. BJ was one of those exceptional guys who knew it early. I have learned far more from my children than I have ever taught them and look forward to the day we are again reunited with BJ.

"There's only me, ain't no equivalent," he said on his Facebook wall, and he was right!

Thank you, Michael, for sharing a part of BJ I didn't know. I know it was painful for you. It will always be painful not having him here, but in reality, it we could only see what we can't see, then we would see all we needed to see.

I love you all eternally!
Mom <3

It's Almost Been a Year Now

So the year is going by since you went away. The Novocain is wearing off, denial far away. Reality now setting in they say time is a healer. But as the clock ticks away it only makes it clearer.

I've come to learn the pain just doesn't go away, not like most folks think it does, who have never felt this way.

You slowly come to terms with it once it's more than you can bear. When it drops you to your knees and you're left in your despair.

Unquenchable this fire inside which never will be put out, but continues to burn a hole in your heart forever without a doubt.

All you can do is learn to live a life never quite the same. To be a different person who forever has been changed. There is no going back, only moving on to tomorrow. Picking yourself up off the floor again, flooded with your sorrow.

If only I could see you now as I know you can see me, I'd have a brighter future of all eternity. But life is bleak without you here, that I can't deny. It's almost been one year now, I have to heal or die. So I'm just living in the moment, just One Day at a Time.

I cannot look behind me the pain is much too real. But moving on without you, I do not want to feel. For one step in each moment, for that I can endure. Just knowing you are happy now, our eternal life is sure.

God grant me the serenity at least another day, to reach a time which surely will come when I too shall be free from pain. I cannot change what's come to pass and so I must accept it. And as homesick as my heart may feel, we'll be reunited yet!

Time

The time passes so slowly, since you've gone away.
Oh how I'd do anything for just another day.

I'm glad you're no longer suffering and the pain you no longer feel. I still am in denial though, can all this really be real?

You were just here last Thanksgiving. Strong and buff as could be. To see the shell of a little boy cancer left of you for me.

In a very short time, and no one had a clue, that in another year, we'd all be missing you.

They say time is a healer of all pain and misery, but I can't see that happening you were just too dear to me.

It hurts to see your pictures and realize you're not here, and to think that time can heal this pain when it's more than I can bear.

JUST DON'T FORGET ME

Your memories will linger on as if it were yesterday. If you were standing by my side, I wonder what you'd say.

You seemed to have a clue that you'd be leaving this earth when, before you even got sick, on your Face Book wall, you talked about it then.

How you hoped that we'd remember you but how could we forget? Such a handsome, giving, caring son who left this world upset.

Still yet to live your Senior year, a family of your own to have. To become a Marine Biologist, your dream snuffed out, so sad.

You would have been the very best had you remained on earth, but I know the Lord had other plans, even before your birth.

Your time to go was all part of His plan; He knew just what He was doing. It's those of us you left behind who struggle to keep on going.

It's so very hard every day when you're all that's on my mind. Even my old activities I've found I've left behind.

I cannot sleep I hardly eat, the emptiness so hollow. If I could have just one last wish you'd be home and well tomorrow.

The Steps

When you feel you can't go on, the denial's really gone. All that's left are your raw feelings, life feels really wrong.

You can't go on another day you simply cannot cope. Now everything is real, you're lost without much hope.

You move onto the next phase and so now anger you must feel at everyone who's in the path, the rage is just unreal.

But mostly you are mad at God, how could He let this be? For He's the only one who could have taken you from me.

So on to bargaining you go, "Please God, I'll do anything you know?" I'll do anything not to feel this pain, oh please just bring him back again.

Trying to negotiate your way out of the hurt, if only this, if only that, but nothing seems to work.

Depression finally sinks in deep. You're drowning in despair. Now realizing he's gone for good and God has taken him there.

The emptiness you feel inside your hollow heart of pain. You withdraw from life left in a fog, intense sadness and despair. You lose interest in what you once loved and find you no longer care.

Acceptance is still the answer to all my pain today. I know I cannot bring you back or make the hurt go away.

So I must readjust to the way my new life is, and learn that things forever change, when a loved one dies.
Nothing will ever be the same you changed my very soul. The love I have inside for you I never will let go.

But I can know that this is how my life is going to be, acceptance is the answer, and acceptance is the key.

It doesn't mean I'm over it or any less do I care. It simply means I'll have to adjust to you no longer being there.

Shattered Dreams

My lifetime dreams now shattered now that you're not here with me, that little boy who held my hand who I no longer see.

God gave you to me for a season then He took your soul away. You must have completed all of the work He gave you on that day.

The day you were brought into my life a joy but gone too soon, though your memories I'll cherish and forever will they bloom.

My heart is utterly broken though I know I'll see you again. But how will I hold myself together from now until then?

Such bittersweet memories I'll hold dear to my heart and forever there you'll stay. You've been gone now for just over 10 months but it seems like just yesterday.

I know you'll be watching over me that you love me and you care. I also know when my time comes you'll be smiling and waiting there.

The love of a Mother for her son will never go away. You'll always be inside my heart forever and a day.

Facebook Post:
March 10, 2013

"You keep the sunshine,
save me the rain"

Alone

So here you sit all alone with nobody there just who do you call when you need somebody to care?

You try to be strong you stumble you fall, you're grasping for air as you're drowning you call. Is anyone out there? You hear nothing at all you're alone.

You think back to the day when your God was your strength, you did nothing at all without kneeling to pray. But the death of your son left you bitter so alone you went on your way.

Now your life full of pride is pulling you down, so you drop to your knees no one else can be found. You turn once again to the Lord you once thought let you down.

Life is so hard you stumble you crawl. You're gasping for air as you're drowning you call, you then realize He never left you at all you're not alone.

You humble yourself and you swallow your pride, you give Him your all in spite of your son who has died, a trust you must build and forever keep Him buy your side.

His son He gave too so that we might all live again, He loves you much more than you can even comprehend. So trust Him and remember to pray daily my friend till the end.

He'll never leave you alone for he'll always be there, in moments of strength and our greatest despair. Just drop to your knees and He'll always be there. Remember my friend, remember Him always in prayer.

Facebook Post:
March 12, 2013

"My new aquarium filter. The Fluval FX5 generates a powerful out-take stream that creates a current that cycles through the tank."

My Little Boy

My little boy what happened, you grew up way too soon. And now instead of happy times I shed a tear or two.

Why did you have to grow up, why couldn't you stay small? I'd wrap you in your blanket and hold you all day long.

You went away to Kindergarten then to Middle school. No matter how big you got you'd say "I love you, too!"

Then into a young man you did become and I soon went away. Leaving you against my will but knowing you wanted to stay.

So off to Utah I did go a happy bride to be. While you and your older brother only once came to visit me.

I thought it would be so much more than me just once a year, to see you only for one week in Houston and you not coming here.

Those times with you were priceless. How much you'll never know. That little boy who grew up, how much I missed I'll never know.

Then soon before your Senior year they told me you were sick. A bug, the flu or something, but we thought you'd get well quick.

The days went on forever, the sickness still remained. All the times we could have had now in my heart refrained.

Soon back to the hospital but this time was to stay. My heart broke every day for you to see you there that way.

Then they told us you had cancer, that baby boy of mine. I just could not believe it, we were running out of time.

Would I have known how short the time we really truly had, I never would have left you with your brother and your dad.

Then I closed my eyes and you were gone completely from my view. So swiftly cancer took your life from everyone you knew,

We had to go on living though the days have all been harder. If only I knew then what I know now, I'd rearrange it and start all over.

So treasure every moment when your loved ones are so near. Because we cannot see around the corner what will soon be clear.

Until the time it happens, until it is too late. Don't live a life full of regrets; love them before it's too late.

My little boy what happened, you grew up way too soon. For you know if I could turn back the clock, I'd happily give you the moon.

Facebook Post:
March 14, 2013

"What's the difference between me and you? I got bacon pancakes."

One of the last text messages between Kelli and BJ:

photo.php?v=424025784355688&comment_id=2611431&offset=0&total_comments=8&notif_t=video_comment have you seen this?

I can't wait to see them! That looks so cool :)

Yeah, I don't want time to disappear, but I want you guys to come down

Disappear?

I don't want time to fly by really fast. Like, I can wait.

About the Author

Kimberly Ann Cutler, first and foremost, is a mom. She is not a writer yet she wrote this book. She is not a poet yet it is filled with poetry. For most of her life raising her six biological children through three different marriages she was a stay-at-home mom by choice until the last eight or so years.

This book was inspired to be written by her seventeen-year-old son, Benjamin Forrest Crawford who lived in the Porter TX, Houston area with his older brother Michael and his father, Norm, after Kimberly divorced him and remarried.

Kimberly now lives in the Salt Lake City area, where she lived previously, when BJ (Benjamin) was nine-months-old until six. Through writing this book she has learned many things about her son she otherwise would have never known.

Some are the many depths and perceptions of the world and this life, BJ's beliefs and what mattered most in life to him. BJ was an old soul in a young body with wisdom beyond his years.

BJ died of T-cell and HLH lymphoma after just three short months but left behind a legacy and

Facebook family on teambj who never will forget him. Two years before his passing he posted on his wall, as he seldom did, about how he wanted to be remembered, how he didn't know how much longer he'd be around, saying he'd stick around for awhile, asking in return, not to be forgotten....as if *he knew*.

His mom, Kimberly, also *knew*. Maybe not before BJ knew it, but through the lyrics of a song when she heard it. This book tells of BJ's short life bundled with happy memories and sad ones. Stories include his wild and funny adventures with friends, his fun loving and caring personality and the complex nature of his very soul.

Though Kimberly is still grieving, with her heart forever broken, changed - she will never be the same again - her faith in God has pulled her through. She believes that everything happens for a reason and God had a greater purpose for her son in another place not so far away as one might think.

She knows without a doubt she will see her beloved son BJ again and until then she leaves him in God's care, whose child BJ really is, and who we all belong to. She dedicates herself in striving to always find new ways to keep BJ's memory alive…Gone but never forgotten! Forever in Our Hearts, We Love You BJ Crawford!

Back Cover: Sirius Fuentes, Michael Crawford (BJ's older brother), Ronnie Grimes

JUST DON'T FORGET ME

www.ingramcontent.com/pod-product-compliance
Lightning Source LLC
Chambersburg PA
CBHW070848050426
42453CB00012B/2093